431
2·592

430
1·009

429
2·553

434
·967

al Chapel

169
5·262

432
2·180

436
5·742

Nant y g
Fa

H·AY

F P

442
12·588

School

443
·219

Police Station

170
·915

Nant y glas dŵr

441
·848

440
1·282

BLACK LION GREEN

445
1·088

R STREET

171
2·064

444
·788

299

446
6·014

Chapel

174
1·517 311

R M 299 3

175
2·521

Methodist Chapel
(Primitive)

Smithy

173
1·206

172
2·527

447

449
1·697

448
·348

Snods Hill

e mawr

176
1·189

246
5·802

R M 309 0

F P

450
2·822

247
1·909

242
8·281

452
·992

Sixpence House

Sixpence House

LOST IN A TOWN OF BOOKS

Paul Collins

BLOOMSBURY

Published by Bloomsbury, New York and London
Distributed to the trade by Holtzbrinck Publishers

Library of Congress Cataloging-in-Publication Data has been applied for.

ISBN 1-58234-284-9

10 9 8 7 6 5 4

First U.S. Edition 2003

Typeset by Hewer Text Limited, Edinburgh
Printed in the United States of America by
RR Donnelley & Sons, Harrisonburg

For Jennifer

Chapter One
Begins Both the Book
and the Journey

I HAVE NEVER noticed the view from the Flatiron Building before. Manhattan, if you tilt your head just right, is a strangely compelling piece of sculpture.

"It's a good thing," my editor says, "that your book isn't being published just now."

"Oh?"

"Because" – he leans forward – "Harry Potter used up all our paper."

"You're joking."

"Seriously."

"No."

He looks at me, a little crestfallen. "I'm telling you the truth. There's two major paper producers for New York publishers, and with a five-million print run of an eight-hundred-page book, well . . . everybody else has to wait in line."

I leaf through the glossies for the photo insert to my book. It has been less than thirty-six hours since I finished writing it on the other side of the continent, in a home that I now no longer own. I was still writing as the movers cleared the furniture out of the apartment, still writing as Jennifer packed the luggage and nursed Morgan to sleep, and as she double-checked that we had my British passport and her and Morgan's visas. I was writing at midnight, at one o'clock, at two o'clock. The computer was the last thing to go into a box, its plastic housing still hot, just five minutes after I had e-mailed the manu-script to my agent.

"So," – I set down the glossies – "publishers are fighting for scraps of paper?"

"So to speak."

Like any editor, he has at least two office walls covered with books; slick stacks of summer catalogs are slipping off his desk; and outside in the editorial department are boxes of books and bound proofs, and yet more walls covered with more books, right down to an incongruous set of old encyclopedias.

A paper shortage? You'd think he'd welcome it.

But one gets the wrong view from the Flatiron Building. For I live in a very small world. So, reader, do you. At this moment, it is just you and I, and it does not matter if you are reading this two hundred years after I have died, or translated into languages unknown to me. We have an understanding. But there are not many of us, and there never have been.

If you grew up in a rural area, you have seen how farmhouses come and go, but the dent left by cellars is permanent. There is something unbreakable in that hand-dug foundational gouge into the earth. Books are the cellars of civilization: when cultures crumble away, their books remain out of sheer stupid solidity. We see their accumulated pages, and marvel – what readers they were!

But were they?

Back in the 1920s, booksellers assessed the core literary population of the United States, the people who could be relied on to buy books with a serious content, at about 200,000 people. This, in a country of 100 million: a ratio of about 500 to 1. It was this minuscule subset spread out over a three-thousand-mile swath, this group of people who could fit into a few football stadiums, that thousands of books released each year had to compete for. Perhaps the ratio has gone higher since then. You see, literary culture is perpetually dead and dying; and when some respected writer discovers and loudly proclaims the finality of this fact, it is a forensic marker of their own decomposition. It means that they have artistically expired within the last ten years, and that they will corporeally expire within the next twenty.

Readers always seem scarce. Before we left San Francisco, my wife and I went on a neighborhood house tour organized by our block association. Our stretch of Waller Street was crammed with Victorian flats, and we all oohed and aahed over each other's wainscoting, box ceilings, and carved mantels. Yet, walking away from the whole thing, stuffed with architecture and potato salad, I felt a nagging doubt.

"Did you notice," I asked my wife, "ours was the only house with books?"

We rounded the corner of Cole, where a broken TV lay in the sidewalk.

"I noticed you made a beeline for their bookcases."

It is the oldest and most incorrigible trait of the booklover.

"Yeah, I know. Here's the thing: all those beautiful built-in bookshelves? They don't hold any books."

And maybe they never did. If you turn the yellowed pages of a volume of *Temple Bar* magazine back to 1881, when these homes were built, you find this:

It really is an APPALLING thing to think of the people who have no books . . . It is only by books that most men and women can lift themselves above the sordidness of life. No books! Yet

3

for the greater part of humanity that is the common lot. We may, in fact, divide our fellow-creatures into two branches – those who read books and those who do not.

Times have not changed much. A recent survey found that half of American households did not buy a single book in the previous year. I knew this statistically, even as I toured my neighbors' houses. And I knew it viscerally when our real estate agent looked around our own flat a few months later.

"You have too many books in here. Home buyers don't like books."

He saw my expression, and shrugged helplessly. "Really. You should hide them."

We did hide them, in the end; we were desperate to leave, because we couldn't afford to live in San Francisco anymore. I tried to imagine a life in the British countryside instead.

"It'll be great" was what I told Jennifer as the Muni bus roared by outside the nursery of our flat. "We'll sell this place, go abroad, and live in an old, old house with old, old books. I'll write books and play piano in the parlor, you'll write books and paint in the garret, and at night . . . we'll drink Horlicks and listen to the BBC."

And then I spread my hands out to indicate what a grand idea it was.

Jennifer pondered this, tapping a pen on a dire bank statement while our son, Morgan, struggled manfully to free himself from his diaper.

"Hay-on-Wye?" she said.

"Yes."

"Hay is a small town."

"Yes."

"Very small."

"Yes."

"You won't miss the U.S.?"

"I won't miss guns."

"That's true."

"Or SUVs."

"Right."

"And Britain has national health."

"Good."

"And the countryside's a good place to be a kid."

"That's true," she said.

"And Hay has a castle right in the middle of town."

"Mmm hmm."

A skateboard rumbles down the pavement outside.

"But," she adds, "if we sell our place here, we can never afford to live in San Francisco again. We can't come back."

"Yeah."

"And we'll have to move all our books."

"Ye – oh, god."

So I went to Haight Mail. Haight Mail is a little shop crammed with PO boxes and copiers off the corner of Masonic, and I had to fax some stuff to my magazine editor anyway. As their fax machine dialed, I tapped my foot and stared at the wall, and then at the store's proprietor.

"You sell shipping boxes, right?"

"Yeah. What are you sending?"

"Books."

"How many?"

I paused to make the calculations. "About . . . two thousand. Maybe three."

His eyebrows rise. "Sent individually?"

"No, no. I'm moving."

"To where?"

"Wales."

He is silent for a long moment. "How," he finally asks, "did you get so many books?"

Well.

I am from Perkiomenville, Pennsylvania, a town so small that it had no traffic lights, no streetlights, no stores, and barely any other kids within walking distance. This gave me lots of time to read. But what I chose to read was a little odd. My parents, being ambitious immigrants – my mother grew up in cramped servants' quarters in Berkshire, my father in Depression-era Liverpool – had bought an outrageously oversize, tumbledown house, and they collected antiques just to fill it up. We'd haunt the auctions of the recently deceased with an old 1940s copy of *Who's Who,* cross-referenced with the estate auction listings in the *Pottstown Mercury.*

"A lawyer from Boston," Mom would note, circling the listing. "I bet he has good furniture."

They'd drag me off on weekends to the bidding. And so there I was, eight years old, in a crowd of sweating, cigar-smoking Pennsylvania Dutchmen, the auctioneer spouting that idiotic bidding dialect over a badly distorting PA. My height placed me exactly at ass level of the crowd, and when I tired of reading the rivets on the seats of their overalls, I'd sneak over to the lunch cart, wolf down a Tastykake, and then sit out on the ruined lawn, where the grass was all pressed down from moving trucks and rugs and cardboard boxes.

"We found a chandelier," my parents might say, dragging a box over to our blue Volvo. But they'd always have found more than that.

Estate-sale boxes never contain just one thing; surviving relatives will empty out the kitchen drawers and the attic trunks into these boxes, because it is better to have bidders pay for your trash than it is to pay for haulers to take it away. Often the lots included old books, which might as well have been trash; nobody ever cared about them.

"Here." Dad would toss me a nineteenth-century chemistry manual. "Something for your room."

I'd leaf through obsolete geology textbooks and forgotten historical romances, and ponder their battered covers and rust-speckled pages. An 1897 edition of *Surface Currents of the Great Lakes* (with diagrams, of course); an undated and strangely compelling, old, board-bound book titled *Great Sea Stories,* with glassine still clinging to the illustrated cover; a rather smelly and stained copy of Gattermann's *Practical Methods of Organic Chemistry* – full of mold spores, appropriately enough. These books held the same fascination for me as the buffalo nickels or mercury dimes that I collected. How did this get here? How did this book, once the pride of a country doctor's library, wind up in an eight-year-old's hands in a forgotten corner of Pennsylvania in 1977?

These books were different from the *Three Investigators* mysteries that I mail-ordered from Scholastic, different from the *Star Trek* novelizations by James Blish that I'd buy from some guy down the road who had a nitrate-saturated chicken coop full of tatty paperbacks. No, these were old. They looked old, they even smelled old. They used old words; the cadences were all wrong, the facts all out-of-date. My most beloved book was a relative youngster: a 1951 volume by Willie Ley called *Rockets, Missiles and Space Travel.* I razored out its atmospheric chart and Scotch-taped it to my wall, next to my giant poster of Doctor J. It showed the highest altitude achieved by any manned vehicle as 72,395 feet. And yet the creamy plate paper, the yellow embossing of a pointy fifties sci-fi rocket on the cover, the feeling of reading Ley's speculation on a moon shot and knowing more than the author did – the true classical sense of irony, where the audience is aware of the ending even as the players of history are not – these things appealed to me in a way that I couldn't explain to my parents or even my best friend.

I have found, rereading Ley's book two decades later, that a number of obscure oddities that turn up in books I have written – the Moon hoax by John Locke, the wondrous book *Mathematicall Magick* published by Bishop Wilkins in 1648, the interplanetary heat ray proposed by Charles Gros – are all described in Ley's volume. I had quietly absorbed these fantastic notions as a child, only to "discover" them again in moldering library books decades later; what I thought was the shock of discovery was, unknown to me, a shock of recognition. It is hard to know just how many times we have been exposed to a word, a face, an idea, before we *have* it. The very idea of an originating point for much of anything becomes hard to pin down. Ley says as much in the words that open his book:

> The story of an idea is, of necessity, the story of many ideas. Ideas, like large rivers, have never just one source. Just as the water of a river near its mouth is composed largely of the waters of many tributaries, so an idea, in its final form, is composed largely of later additions. And because this is so, it is often difficult to find the source of a river or the beginnings of an idea.

The same might be said of this book. I wrote it; my name is on the title page. But it did not entirely come from me: it is from many writers, and many books, without a clear starting point. I couldn't even tell you how this book really began.

Chapter Two
Relies on the Travelogue Cliché
of a Garrulous Cabdriver

WHEN I LEFT MY publisher's office in Manhattan, the city was stinking hot, and so I assumed that – of course – London would be just as hot. Now I am shivering out on Queensway and trying to find a cab. Instead, an overloaded truck lumbers past, its sides emblazoned:

> *Bowsley Brothers*
> *Crispy Bacon Specialists*

Jennifer and Morgan, at least, are still sheltered in our hotel room; I'm out working on my own for the day, leaving my wife to ponder how best to get a baby and stroller over to the Tate Modern.

Eventually I succeed in hailing a stout and shiny black taxi. I slide in across the backseat.

"Great George Street."

I do not know where Great George Street is, but I gather from the name that it is a short and narrow street, on which no person named George has ever resided.

"Where on Great George?"

"The Institute of Civil Engineers."

I rifle through my notes. We have to spend the day in London before going to Hay, because I'm paying for this leg of the family exodus by writing a piece for an American tech magazine on retrostructures. This is a word I have made up. I am very good at coining neologisms when free plane tickets are involved. Retrostructures are, you see, old infra*structures retro*fitted for fiber optics. This, at least, is what I told the magazine. I do not mention that, before the meeting, the word did not exist.

"You know where to find these . . . *retrostructures*?" an editor asked.

Oh, my, yes, I told him. Why, London is crawling with them.

The cabbie's gray eyes observe me in the mirror. "So you're not out for the Queen Mum?"

"What?"

"Queen Mum." The cab dodges another barricade of fluorescent-vested officers waving us around. "It's her hundredth birthday. Lots of streets closed – including yours, I gather."

And yet we reach it.

"They're predicting big crowds today, for a parade or something," he adds. "But I expect the Queen Mum will be disappointed."

I look out the window: he's right. The masses who have not shown up for the Millennium Dome are not showing here either. The street is empty, save for hundreds of police, walking with hands clasped behind their backs, looking quite stern in their black, tit-headed helmets. The only civilian is a single forlorn custodian, who stands with his rubbish stick at the ready. He is waiting to spear the first crumpled crisps packet that flutters out of some pensioner's string bag.

Mr. Thomas, an engineer for Cable & Wireless, is showing me around the Institute library. Their library is quite lovely, tall-ceilinged and echoey, replete with old books on hydraulics and steam-valve fittings. The building is old and marble and wooden, a heroic structure from the steam age of Brunel and Bessemer, back when civil engineering seemed miraculous.

It is hard to imagine today the utter difference between a Victorian structure and our own. We can effortlessly manufacture sheets of glass that will dwarf a man, and steel beams stronger and purer than what anyone in Brunel's age could have dreamed of. Structure becomes pliable, plastic. And within those structures you really have plastic, infinitely moldable and colored. To walk into one of these old buildings is to wonder: can you imagine building a computer, or a refrigerator, out of wood and stone? It is an entirely different realm of materials and all the parameters that limit them. And they have a different touch and smell; I can recognize the sweetish smell of steam heating and old wood benches, and I think of myself back in my old school, sitting in chapel and staring at the memorial names of past students from the classes of 1917 and 1918 on the opposite wall, all killed off by war and influenza.

"I must go now," Thomas tells me as I pore over the minutes from an old engineering conference. "But you might want to know, it's just a rumor, but I hear there's fiber cable laid alongside the old Regent's Canal."

After photocopying some declassified reports about a WWII repair made on the Tower Tunnel – a pedestrian tunnel built under the Thames, next to the Tower of London, which became so overrun with hookers and pickpockets that it was closed down and converted to a giant utility conduit – I proceed out of the Institute and down a few random streets, hugging my body against the cold and looking for a shop where I can buy an A to Z map to London. The map's creator, Phyllis Pearsall, first moved to London in 1935, after a divorce, thinking she'd become a portrait painter. And so she did; but of a place, rather than a person.

"Sir?"

A bobby is looking at me inquisitively.

I stop walking; the access is blocked. It is Downing Street.

"Ah." I nod and move on.

Once I find a map and provision myself at a Boots with a pickle sandwich, a squeeze box of Ribena, and a disposable camera, I'm ready to go infrastructure hunting. I sit on a cold stone bench in front of a monument and thumb through the A to Z, then pore over a Tube map so miniaturized that it resembles a circuit board. The canal, it turns out, is near King's Cross, a station I have been to many times to use the British Library. But when I finally disembark at the tube stop – minding the gap – I resist the pull of the library. This time I turn the opposite corner and immediately know that I am not in Tourist Approved London anymore. The street smells like it is paved with kidney stones. About half the buildings are boarded up, and the few stores left open have hand-lettered signs. There is no Queen Mum here. There are no bearskin-helmeted guards. One block of flats has sunken front garden plots, or what had once been garden plots, now stuffed several feet deep with fast-food wrappers. Old brickpile factories stare vacantly, and in the distance the empty skeleton of a gasworks looms over the river.

I step gingerly down to the canal's towpath. A group of men are sitting by the riverside fishing and drinking imported Budweisers from a cooler.

"Afternoon," one greets me cheerily with a tip of his beer.

I look at the scummy water. "What are you fishing for?"

"Dinner," says another.

I walk on; a few ducks paddle peacefully around the plastic bags floating in the water; ivy crawls around the grimy old brick walls facing the canal, sprouting out of crumbling holes that once held valves and overflow pipes. It all feels slightly sad, like those long stretches of dead-mill brickshells encrusting the Amtrak line in Virginia, the overgrown ruins of old factories so plaintive that it just makes you want to move to Athens, Georgia, and start a band.

I sometimes wonder whether century-old ruins look so beautiful to us because they were *meant* to ruin in a beautiful way. There was a Romantic fascination with structural decay; wealthy gentry had custom-built ruins erected on their estates, their own little Country Churchyards to elegize in. And so in a time when many stonemasons were engaged with increasingly elaborate cities of the dead, lavishly constructed urban cemeteries where only pestilential graveyards once stood, soon you get architects thinking of decay too.

There is, in San Francisco, a beautiful spot not far off the Golden Gate Bridge, the Palace of Fine Arts. It is an echoing rotunda and a set of classical columns projecting up before a calming pond; it seems so at odds with the wooden California architecture all around it that the effect is startling, like Kirk and his landing party stumbling upon a Roman temple on an alien planet's surface. Not so many years ago, before I met my wife or found gainful employment, I'd crash on a friend's floor in the Marina, wake at no particular hour, and walk over to that pond, armed with a mug of coffee that I'd swiped from the kitchen, and prepare for my doctoral exams with a rubber-band-bound stack of index cards filled with Latin vocabulary. I'd stare at the columns across the water and wonder how they'd landed there. Like the ablatives and vocatives of Latin that I was struggling through, they belonged in another land and place altogether.

But it was no accidental ruin. Their architect, Bernard Maybeck, built them out of a burlap and plaster mixture as part of a huge building complex for the 1915 Panama-Pacific International Exposition. It was designed to look like a ruin in every sense: the columns are hollow, and Maybeck wanted vines to grow inside and around, and water to flow like tears from the faces of maidens depicted beneath the dome. The tendrils of the plants and the wear of the water would destroy the complex, and San Franciscans could watch the structure self-destruct before their eyes. Maybeck was talked out of these details, but it hardly mattered: the Palace unraveled through neglect anyway, and by World War II the ruined columns towered over an army parking lot full of jeeps.

Not long afterward, Maybeck was asked how the ruined ruin should be restored. Plant redwoods, he helpfully advised:

> Redwoods grow fast, you know. And as they grow, the columns of the rotunda would slowly crumble, at approximately the same speed. Then I would like to design an altar, with the figure of a maiden praying, to install in that grove of redwoods. I should like my Palace to die behind those great trees of its own accord, and become its own cemetery.

Maybeck, I imagine, appreciated his London contemporaries in this regard. H. G. Wells spent a good part of his *War of the Worlds* methodically destroying England, slashing its entire landscape into a ruin of terrible beauty – and then lived long enough to see the Luftwaffe cruelly realize his fantasy in every British urban center. And when his Time Machine travels forward to mysterious ruins, the Time Traveller finds an enigmatic museum, abandoned, filled with broken displays of artifacts. The repository of the ruined past becomes a past ruin itself.

Their magazines used to be full of this stuff. All this was being written when the British Empire was at its absolute zenith, owner of a quarter of the world's landmass, and decades before any world war would sap away its vitality. I cannot think of any other empire that, as it encircled the world, had so many artists pondering how it would look in its decrepitude.

Back then, even the new buildings felt like ruins in the making.

There is a wonderful old travelogue on Britain that the American journalist J. M. Bailey published in 1879, *England Through the Back Door*. It's long forgotten now, but I'm fond of it, and not simply because it concludes with a full paragraph transcription of the author barfing on the Channel ferry.* It's because of paragraphs like this on London:

> There are occasionally new buildings, – the most of them going up on the old plan, just as their forefathers would have done it. When you see a new stone building (when you do, remember), you see something that involuntarily moves you to tears. The stone is of a streaked, yellowish-brown tint, – such a tint as rusting and weeping iron imparts to marble; and, to a stranger who has a guide-book in every pocket, it is a spectacle that sends hot blood flying to his head, and makes every nerve tingle. It looks like a building dug out of an ancient peat-bed; and how often have I seen new Americans leaning up against them and crying, and policemen hustling them away!

Even in jest, how often do we react that way to a new home now? Drywall and veneered particleboard do not exactly put you in the presence of the sublime; most building materials today will not age gracefully and were never meant to. They are only meant to be new. Perhaps the ancient brick walls in London weren't built with much more foresight for their aesthetic future than any structure today; yet by their very nature they succeed perfectly as ruins.

I spend more hours wandering through Whitechapel, looking for old industrial buildings that are abandoned or being turned into lofts,

---

* Which reads: "Wh-hoop! – whoooo – whoooo – who-oop! Oh, dear! ———— whoooo – whoooo – whooo-oooo-oop! Mercy on me! Wh-hoop! wh-hoop! whooooo-oop! Heav – wh-whoop! (Pause of a moment.) Oo-oo-oo-oo-ooh – wh-hoop! – wh-hoop – wh-hoop!"

peering up their redbrick sides for pipes and valve boxes marked LHPC – short for the London Hydraulic Power Company. The pipes are used as fiber-optic conduits now, blasting through the force of a million words a moment, but they used to pump water all over industrial London at 700 psi – the kind of pressure that saws fingers off when it leaks. Until 1977, when what little industry was left in Britain used electric motors anyway, everything from dock cranes to department-store freight elevators were powered by these lines. Nobody cares about them now, apart from a few industrial historians, which is why I'm wandering in weedy lots strewn with rubble. It's a crummy neighborhood, and I feel as if this should be dangerous; and so it would be, if there were another human being in sight. But the only danger here is tripping on a piece of broken macadam. I make a few last desultory passes through the block where I hear an LHPC pumphouse once stood, then move on to look for another bit of infrastructure off King's Road.

It's not there anymore. If I wanted to see a recycled power plant, I'd have been better off going to the Tate with Jennifer and Morgan. I am mostly wasting my time today, it seems, chasing a past that has been buried and recycled and scrapped out of existence. And worse still, nobody seems to remember these things anymore; the extraordinary thing about time is that it will engulf large objects almost as quickly as small ones.* What past there is to find here is only for sale, and out of my price range; for there are some nice antiquarian booksellers along King's Road. I enter one of them: there are neatly arrayed leatherbound volumes crammed tightly into shelves, like barricades of words to keep any actual readers out. There are no paperbacks here, no stained cloth bindings. It is not that kind of

---

* When the Boston Theatre was torn down in 1926, an entire two-story house was found underneath a staircase.

bookstore. The clerk, in the back, is listening to Radio 2 and is quite happy to ignore me.

Leatherbound books are an expensive form of wallpaper, and yet every English nobleman's home seems to have had them. Their endless sets of the works of Cooper and Scott and Goethe, in finely tanned bindings with marbled endpapers, all end up with this sort of dealer sooner or later. I look through a set of Cooper and, without surprise, find uncut pages: these books were never actually read.

They also have, I see, a book inscribed by Gladstone. I do not recognize the title, and it means little to me, for I have never quite understood the appeal of books that had famous owners. Unless they made copious notes in them, what's the point? To have a dealer deliver up a famously owned book to you, where's the fun in that? The real thrill, if there is any, would be in finding such signatures yourself. I have only ever discovered one such inscription. The book was given to Herb Caen, the last of the Runyonesque reporters, who wrote in the *San Francisco Chronicle* about his beloved "Baghdad by the Bay" with an unparalleled mastery of the dot-dot-dot; a guy from the generation that wore snappy hats, for whom a martini at lunch was not an affectation. Not long before Caen died, I was pawing through a sidewalk blanket seller's stock in North Beach and came across this cast-off book given to him by some grateful reader; written neatly inside the cover, it read, "Hope you enjoy this as much as I did!"

The book was a history of toilet plumbing.

Chapter Three
Skips a Tiring Train Journey
and Alights in the Welsh Countryside

I love Hay.

It has been two years since our last visit; Morgan was still gestating. The first time we came here, about four years ago, it was simply to kill a couple loose days in our travel schedule as we toured around Britain; the *Lonely Planet* guide singled out Hay-on-Wye, a place I'd never heard of before, as a mecca for booklovers in general, and antiquarian-book collectors in particular.

"Well," I'd said, *"that sounds like the place for me."*

We stayed on a cobblestone side street at a little B&B called Jasmine Cottage, and that summer the house was living up to its fragrant name. It was run by a hospitable older couple, the Johnsons. In the morning, after nearly getting exfoliated by the first decent water pressure in weeks, I would go downstairs and see them in their breakfast room. There they'd heap sausages and tomatoes and mushrooms in front of me, while regaling me with stories of their travels, the strange local folk, and how Hay had broken off from Britain once to declare independence.

"Someday," Mr. Johnson said, "you shall have to meet the King of Hay."

He and Mrs. Johnson laughed, and I did too; but they laughed harder.

The town we found that first day was filled with stores stuffed to the rafters with old books, massive ancient shelfbreakers like a *Pilgrim's Progress* the weight and color of a manhole cover, a heavy bit of allegory indeed; and a slim and beautiful copy of *Eve's Diary* – a curiously innocent work, lush with languid Beardsley-like drawings on every page, almost unrecognizable as being by Mark Twain, of all people – we spent hundreds of pounds just shipping them all back home. At the end of our visit we loaded our bags into the taxi and drove away, both a little sad to leave. The hedgerows and dappled light sped past as our vehicle wound its way to Hereford.

"When I am old," I said to Jennifer, "that is where I want to retire."

We'd paid about £25 a night for this. It was amazing. And so we made sure to come back again the next year, in the middle of a bitter winter. But we couldn't go back, it turned out. The cottage phone was disconnected, the jasmine hidden under snow, and the Johnsons themselves . . . vanished.

We had ended up calling another local inn, the Seven Stars. The owner, Mary Ratcliffe, answered the phone.

"We're arriving on New Year's Day," my wife explained. "Will you have any rooms then?"

"Barely," Mary said, laughing. "We just bought the place. You'll be our first customers."

It has been three years since that first stay at the Seven Stars, but it all looks just the same on the long drive from Hereford station – winding through the apple orchards and rapeseed fields, the sleepy little single-lane bridge by the old vicarage of Bredwardine, and the mansion of, yes, those Baskervilles – down past endless miles of hedgerows, the Tudor houses by the road, and castellated medieval towers that still loom over old cornfields.

Our taxi roars around the curve and into Hay – Y Gelli, the sign informs us, for we have just crossed the Welsh border. The buildings in this part of town are low and stony, as if they have been pounded down by a giant mallet. The cab's tires are rumbling now; the streets turn crooked and cobblestoned, and the buildings close in over us.

The taxi stops at the Seven Stars, and we emerge to toss down our bags in a courtyard fringed with flowers. It is late July: bees are buzzing drowsily in the roses. The Ratcliffes emerge from the kitchen, their collie Major bounding after them.

I feel an overwhelming and sudden sense of relief.

"You're back!" Mary says, and we smile.

"We *are* back," Jennifer replies. "And maybe for good."

Our room has a little electric kettle – every British traveler's room does – and Jennifer is boiling tea and arranging Bourbon cream biscuits on a dish while I unpack. You have read of elaborate Japanese tea ceremonies. There is a certain lack of decorum in the British ceremony, particularly when you wind the bit of string around your Typhoo bag to strain out the last bits of brown juice, then whip the sodden little paper mess into the rubbish bin. The British now spend more on coffee than tea anyway. And yet there is indeed a mystery to tea in this country.

No situation is so dire that it cannot be interrupted for tea. It is particularly important to the British when it is cold and damp outdoors, which is often, or when it is cold and damp indoors, which is always. The most transcendent passage on tea in the English language is from outdoors, though, in Jerome K. Jerome's *Three Men in a Boat*. The tale of three bachelors in their late twenties venturing out onto a river should be, I think, an entire genre unto itself. I was at that precise place in life when I first read the book. My old roommate Mike introduced me to it by reading aloud this passage in which the

three men have settled down to tea after boiling a kettleful of river
water:

> We had made the tea, and were just settling down comfortably
> to drink it, when George, with his cup halfway to his lips,
> paused and exclaimed:
> "What's that?"
> "What's what?" asked Harris and I.
> "Why that!" said George, looking westward.
> Harris and I followed his gaze, and saw, coming down
> towards us on the sluggish current, a dog. It was one of the
> quietest and peacefullest dogs I have ever seen. I have never
> met a dog who seemed more contented – more easy in its
> mind. It was floating dreamily on its back, with its four legs
> stuck up straight in the air. It was what I should call a full-
> bodied dog, with a well-developed chest. On he came, serene,
> dignified, and calm, until he was abreast of our boat, and
> there, among the rushes, he eased up, and settled down cosily
> for the evening.
> George said he didn't want any more tea, and emptied his
> cup into the river. Harris did not feel thirsty either, and
> followed suit. I had drunk half mine, but wished I had not.

This may be the only instance in recorded literature of Englishmen
not finishing their tea; for this is a country where citizens will not
grumble or take action at much of anything unless it interferes with
their cup. Some years ago, a species of English tit bird discovered that
if they pecked through the foil cap on milk bottles, they could suck
down a cream feast so sumptuous that they could barely stagger away
afterward on their little bird feet. Other varieties of tits quickly
learned by watching, and suddenly the nation's cream tea was in

mortal peril; whereupon redesigned bottle caps were procured with impressive alacrity.

Perhaps it is not always cold and damp indoors; despite the chill over London yesterday, I wake up from my jet-lagged nap in the early evening covered in sweat – I am in the top story of an old building on what has become a hot day. Everyone else is already up; Jennifer is arranging the little tubes of acrylic paint that she had crammed into Tupperware containers for the flight over, and Morgan has discovered that our hotel room has sheer white curtains. He toddles behind them, drapes them over his face like a bride, sways from side to side, and then staggers forward to feel the fabric running out over his skin.

We pull on our clothes to venture outside. The Seven Stars Inn is at a T-intersection of Broad Street and Chancery Lane; to one side is the town center, marked by the clock tower. A tractor rumbles past, heading out of town and toward the countryside. The farm fields start just a few hundred yards away. But from here, all you can see are crooked old buildings crammed with booksellers.

Hay-on-Wye, you see, is *The Town of Books.* This is because it has fifteen hundred inhabitants, five churches, four grocers, two newsagents, one post office . . . and forty bookstores. *Antiquarian* bookstores, no less. And they are in antiquarian buildings: there are scarcely any buildings in Hay proper that are under a hundred years old; not many, even, that are under two hundred years old. There are easily several million books secreted away in these stores and in outlying barns around the town; thousands of books for every man, woman, child, and sheepdog – first editions of Wodehouse, 1920s books in Swahili, 1970s books on macramé, pirated Amsterdam editions of Benjamin Franklin's treatise on electricity, and maybe even a few unpulped copies of John Major's autobiography.

It was not always so: in the 1960s Hay was a declining market town, a cheese-and-eggs-and-butter anachronism of Saturday markets in a new era of lorry transport and supermarkets. But it was an ancient place with a ancient purpose, for it straddles the natural border of the river Wye, delineating England and Wales – buy your rhubarb at the Spar Market, and you're buying it in Wales; buy it down the road at the Pioneer Co-op, and you are buying it in England – and so it has been a place of war and military fortification ever since the English and the Welsh first decided to clobber each other. Which is to say, forever. The Black Mountains around it are dotted with Neolithic arrowheads and Bronze Age barrows, and the riverbank sediment hides the remains of a Celtic community and a late Roman camp. There have been castles here for a thousand years; the first one was burned down in 1216 after the local baron, having rather miffed King John, was walled up alive in Windsor Castle to starve to death. Hay Castle has been built and destroyed repeatedly and local nobility slaughtered many times since then, for the British do love to keep up old traditions; and the current owner of Hay Castle – now an imposing rockpile that towers on a hill over the center of town – did his bit for tradition when most of the building was gutted in a conflagration in 1978.

And yet the owner of the castle is also largely responsible for the creation of Hay in its modern form. He is a very curious fellow by the name of Richard Booth, and when he showed up to buy the town's Old Fire Station in 1962, he was a brash young Oxford lad, eager to do something different from his classmates. So he became a shopkeeper. At first he was selling books and, well, *antiques*. Of a sort. One of the antiques for sale, a miniature port barrel, had been in his shop window for a week before he was gently informed that it was brand-new and could be purchased at a pub down the street.

Believe it or not, Booth is now the most powerful man in Hay.

We walk into the town's one Chinese restaurant, our eyes adjusting to dim light. There are no tables, no chairs, just a take-away counter and an old linoleum floor, though it was once clearly meant to be a dining area. Two sofas are on either side of the empty room, and you have nothing to stare at except for whoever is sitting on the opposite couch. Jennifer and I wait there for our takeout, receive it in silence, and then walk back out into the sunlight beating down upon the cobblestones, our weighty bags of dinner in hand.

The town has quieted in the early evening, and we have the road largely to ourselves. I carry Morgan on my shoulders up Church Street, and we pass by a big old rise in the earth, universally known here as The Tump, all that remains of the original castle from – I don't know, a thousand years ago? – overlooking the river.*

I want to play in the churchyard ahead, amid the tombstones. There is nothing odd in this. They have cemeteries in Britain like they have corn in Iowa. Morgan, whose great love in life is opening and closing doors, scrambles around the big, heavy iron gate of St. Mary's in his funny stumble-walk, a little man drunk on air. He smiles at us as he pushes the cemetery gate shut.

Right by St. Mary's is a sign pointing off the road:

The Warren
Waterfall

---

* No one that I ask in Hay seems to know what this ancient name means; but at length I came across the word *tymp* in an old Welsh dictionary. It means "mound." How wonderfully droll our ancestors were.

And down the path we go. It starts paved and sunny but soon turns dark and wild; thistles everywhere, poor-man's orchids, bracken, brambles, and the sound of the waterfall rushing by below. Past that, through the trees, you can see sparkles of water – the river Wye. Every few yards a bird comes flushing out of the bushes, startling us as we startle them. I can hear them hoo-hooing across the field at each other, and a rook cawing.

"This is great."

"It is."

We sit down on a bench to munch the egg rolls. They are the size of burritos, and the sweet-and-sour sauce tastes of beer.

Running straight along the upper elevations of the steep river embankment is a solid dirt path, with remarkably few roots to trip you up. There are, at intervals, stout stone arches at its side, seemingly leading to nowhere. It was some years after I first came to Hay that I discovered that this path is the remains of a railroad. It ran steam trains from Hereford to Hay, and onward to Brecon; rail company directors used to hold meetings in the Swan Hotel, and the tackle-and-camping-goods shop that stands today on Belmont Street was once a railroad ticket office. It had never occurred to me that the overgrown path leading down past the side of the shop had ever been anything other than a long driveway; but once, it was for a horse-drawn tram pulling cargo up from and down to the train.

The world is full of such things: remnants that give no clue of their origin, that no one would think to question as ever having been anything but what they now are. The first house that I knew growing up in Perkiomenville was quite small, and the oldest in the township, dating back to the 1720s. My nursery was tiny – even at the age of three, it seemed so to me – and it had no windows. But it, like me, hadn't even existed a few years before. My parents had noticed that the exterior dimensions of the house and the interior dimensions did not match and attacked a wall with crowbars to uncover the discrepancy. Peering inside the cavity with flashlights, they found the skeletal remains of a big water tank; it had probably been empty for two hundred years, and the dried boards had shriveled so much that there were one-inch gaps between each plank. With these planks torn out, the emptied space could just accommodate my crib.

I revisited that house about twenty years later. The current owners didn't know that the little room had been nonexistent for hundreds of years, or that it had once been someone's sleeping quarters. They were using it as a broom closet, and I imagine the next owners will too.

Chapter Four
Looks for a Place
to Call Its Own

JENNIFER AND I have been quietly watching the Clee Tompkinson offices for months; or rather, watching their on-line real estate listings. We have had our eye on a tall and beautiful old building, one that I have been in before – the Verso Bookshop, which is across Broad Street from the Seven Stars Inn. Peering out the inn's window this morning and squinting my eyes at the shop, I can see the FOR SALE sign is still up in its window. Good. Nobody has jumped our chance to make a bid.

I sit back down at the breakfast table.

"Thinking of buying the Verso?" Mary asks as she sets out the toast.

"We've an appointment with the estate agent today."

"We might be neighbors then!"

"I hadn't thought of that." I raise my cup of tea. "Well, to neighborliness, then."

"I should ask Mr. Ratcliffe about that building first, though," she confides. "I'm not really from here, you know. But he is. He can tell you about the buildings around here. He's probably been in every one of them."

I have the table to myself as I tuck into the breakfast – Jennifer is not really a breakfast person, and neither, apparently, is anyone else in the inn today – and once I have digested a little, had my tea, and tossed a thumbed-over *Guardian* onto the seat next to me, I am ready to go househunting. As I get up to leave the room, Mary reappears and waves me over.

"Just so you know," she half-whispers, "I spoke with my husband."

"About the bookshop?"

Mary nods gravely. "One of the adjoining houses, when they put in the central heating, all the windows in the Verso fogged up. It was that damp inside."

"Well. That means it's authentic."

"Martin Like," I tell my wife as we hoist up Morgan and leave the inn. "That's the agent I talked to on the phone." There are only five or six family names in Hay, and Like is one of them. You can walk into any shop here and demand to see Mr. Like, or perhaps a Mrs. Davies, and someone by that name will almost certainly stir to help you.

Martin's office is in a part of town known as the Bull Ring; a hundred years ago, open-air china markets used to be held there. Now it's just another intersection. We stare at the listings in the estate agent's window, knowing that they are watching us from the inside, waiting for us to come in. We enter the office a little timidly.

"Hi. We're looking for a house." I say this as if a house has grown legs and bolted from the paddock.

A flustered young man bolts up from his desk and shakes our hands nervously. "You're the fellow who called from San Francisco?"

"Yes, that's me."

"I'm Martin, Martin Like."

He is a nice, stammering, bespectacled fellow, for Britain is a realm of nice stammering fellows: Hugh Grant has immortalized them for all posterity.

"So, I'm guessing from your name," my wife says, "that you're from Hay."

"Yes, yes, indeed I am, yes." Martin gathers up a sheaf of house descriptions, and a survey map of the town. "I lived away from here for a while, but I was pulled back."

"It pulled us back."

"Yes." He smiles. "Hay has that effect on people."

There is a strange pause.

"Shall we go see the Verso Bookshop?" he says.

"We're dying to."

What used to be the Verso Bookshop can be reached by a back street of fieldstone houses, Chancery Lane. To enter the bookshop storefront, everyone cuts across a neighbor's lawn, which has been so worn from such ill-usage over the centuries that it has largely been replaced by small paving stones.

The building is perhaps three hundred or four hundred years old, with a whitewashed exterior and the feel of musty, low-beamed age in its storefront. It has a new bookseller tenant, a temporary one taken in after the Verso Bookshop left. Though the store is left open, the tenant is gone right now, even as the chatter of radio continues to address him in his absence.

"Hello?" Martin yells. "Is anybody in?"

The radio mutters on.

"I guess we have the place to ourselves for now." Martin smiles. "Let's see if we can get into the house."

We walk through the grim storefront, spring a locked door at the back, and then duck below a phone line that has been strung diagonally across the doorway. Heavy oak floorboards creak beneath our feet, and threadbare Orientals cover the floors in front of us; immediately to our left is a dark and crowded stairwell. This is a weighty structure, the sort of moany old house under constant compression by the very years themselves; it is not airy.

"This is the entrance," Martin says. "Let's go back into the kitchen."

The kitchen, like a bizarrely high proportion of British kitchens that I have seen, is distinctly of 1950s vintage; you half expect an Angry Young Man with a Yorkshire accent to step out and start yelling about working down in *the bloody mines*. The backyard is reached through this kitchen, and it is weedy and overgrown with nettles; looking up, I realize that a neighboring restaurant looks down into the yard. So, no naked revels then.

"This house is owned by a book dealer, so you'll have to step around a few piles of stock," Martin says as he leads us back in to the stairs.

"Which shop does he run?"

"I'm not sure that he actually has a shop here," Martin admits. "I think he's more an intermediary for bringing remainders to various stores."

This had never really occurred to me. Hay seems like a town run by solitary eccentrics with their little bookstores, and yet there must be a secondary economy built around their needs, and mostly peopled by artisans, middlemen, and laborers; all, I'm sure, of vastly greater sense and practicality than the booksellers themselves.

We ascend a frighteningly steep staircase, holding Morgan tight and dodging little stacks of doomed cookbooks and glossy stiffs meant for the coffee table. The tenant is clearly not a risk-averse fellow, for remainders are a dodgy business proposition and always have been. I once found a charming book bearing the mysterious title *Sunwise Turn;* it proved to be a 1923 account by Madge Jenison of her

Fifth Avenue bookshop of the same name. Jenison was the kind of person who would lecture a customer on why he had to read *The Theory of the Leisure Class* by Thorstein Veblen, only to discover later that the customer was, in fact, Thorstein Veblen.

She'd started up the shop without any previous experience in bookselling or retailing at all and began by buying a stack of remaindered books just like these littering the stairs:

> In that first buy were one hundred copies of *Hunting Indians in a Taxicab* . . . an account of how a woman made a collection of cigar store Indians that used to stand in front of the little news and stationery and tobacconist stores fifty years ago. You found a new model only once in a blue moon, and then you dashed away in a taxicab and returned with it for your gallery. My partner and I could see ourselves selling it hand over hand – it delighted us to its last scratch of ink. It was a remainder and we bought one hundred at 10¢ a copy and planned to sell it at $1 a copy. It seemed a scandal to us that such an amusing book should go out of print. *Hunting Indians* grew to be the joke of the shop, and we pinned a medal on the breast of anyone who sold one.

Come to think of it, perhaps the fellow living here has done well for himself – for the middleman who sold the remainders to Jenison was surely the only one to ever make any money off *Hunting Indians in a Taxicab*.

"So how long has he been here?"

"Not terribly long."

"Hmm."

"I don't think he's moving so soon because of the house itself," Martin quickly adds.

"How long has it been for sale?"

"Since November."

"Hmm."

There is no denying that in some ways the house is quite beautiful. It is full of low, recessed windows that look out over Broad Street and past the golden fields and the river that lie beyond. A wobbly ladder leads up into a loft that was once nothing but slate and ancient beams, and it's now disgustingly particleboarded-up. With the alleged improvements torn away, though, it could be interesting.

But that's true of the entire house. Every room needs remodeling; the current owner's only done one bathroom and given up after that. Probably got in over his head. Which means, of course, that we would most certainly be in over ours. And the near-vertical staircase and the low windows would spell certain death for Morgan.

From five thousand miles away, this house looked like *it*. But now . . .

"Here's the sale sheet," Martin says, handing it to me. "The price has been reduced."

And indeed it has. But it still has *money pit* written all over it.

"So," Jennifer tells Martin as we walk back down Chancery Lane, "we will need an agent in our house search."

Martin takes off his glasses, wipes them, and utters "Ah!" under his breath. "I'd forgotten. You have agents for buying in America, don't you?"

"Well, yes. Of course."

"Yes, yes, well, we only have them for *selling* here, you see."

We stare blankly at him.

"Buyers," he adds, "do not have representation. Only sellers do."

"So we have no one to look out for us?"

"Not as such, no. I will be happy to give advice, of course." He opens the office door to us. "But you will need to keep in mind that, strictly speaking, I am representing the seller's interests."

The British system of property selling is medieval in a literal sense; there are no MLS listings here, no system of termite and roofing and lead-paint inspections. Sellers are not obliged to reveal defects in the house, so that you have to play a game of twenty questions – a hundred is more like it – just to make sure the house is not about to fall off a cliff or collapse into an ancient cesspool.

And then there is gazumping. Contracts in Britain are not binding until almost the moment you move in. And so the seller can gazump – that is, if another buyer offers more money for the house, even as you are packing the moving van, the seller can suddenly demand more money, or the deal is off.

The buyer can screw the seller this way too. This is called gazundering.

The estate agent, not liking either buyer or seller, can also decide to pull out of the deal. This is called gazurping.

No, sorry. I made that last word up – I *think*.

But this part is quite true: the ancient terms on land are binding. If your household was once required to give a roasted boar and a bushel of millet to the local vicar every winter solstice . . . it still might be.

We promise to see Martin again later that week, and as the afternoon winds down, Jennifer and I push Morgan in his stroller out to Warren Close. It's past St. Mary's churchyard, and the houses are much cheaper out here.

We cross the road to stop in a little corner shop. A cream slice is temptingly displayed on the counter. Let me explain the cream slice: it is a slab of pastry loaded with an absurd stack of thick double cream. If they had regulations for building pastries, no cream slice would ever come up to code. You'd always have to pay off the inspector. A cream slice will invariably collapse onto your shirt; which this one promptly does on mine. I don't care. It is a very good cream slice.

We reach Warren Close and examine the outside. Not bad, but the houses are newish, and they all kind of look the same. It is a typical British middle-class development: brownstone, neatly trimmed hedges, tiny gardens. Kids speed around on trikes and silvery scooters. And it all looks like . . . well, a suburb.

"We didn't have to leave California for this."

One child passes by on his bike; he is maybe eight years old. We are often accosted by small British children. I don't know why. My entire memory of a trip to Ludlow consists of a girl skipping behind us with a newly bought pound-loaf, singing, *Crusty bread, crusty bread, crusty crusty crusty bread*.

"Are you lost?" this boy says.

"No. We're just looking to buy a house."

"You going to buy that one?" He points at one for sale, indistinguishable from the rest on the street.

"Maybe. We don't know."

He cycles off.

"It's ugly inside!" he yells back.

Chapter Five
Goes Bookhunting

WE'VE BEEN IN THE Seven Stars for several days, and we need something more permanent.

"I'll take care of it," Jennifer says, and carefully puts the accommodations listings on top of a Milton Bradley box. "But first, it is very important that I finish this puzzle."

The day is hot, so stifling that Morgan is slumped into an early nap, and Jennifer is keeping indoors to do her jigsaw of an alpine meadow. So I am on my own outdoors, walking down the melting streets to Hay Print and Design, which is the only place in town to get online access.

CLOSED

I give the door a little push, in disbelief, and it won't budge. Closed, at eleven-thirty? I peer at the sign in the darkened window. On Tuesday they're closed all afternoon and reopen at five. This should not really surprise me in rural Britain. Theirs is not a twenty-four-hour economy. It's barely even a six-hour economy. Stores close early and often, and if you want anything after then – well, you shouldn't want anything after then. You should go home, eat supper, and watch the Beeb.

There is, at least, the possibility of doing some bookhunting.

Richard Booth owns the two biggest bookstores in town: the Castle, and The Limited, a massive old factory here on Lion Street, the front of which is set in with tiles depicting farm activities. It was a farm machinery works, once. I have not gone into either store yet; I want to pick off a smaller one first to sharpen my hunting skills.

I sweat and shamble uphill on a shortcut known as The Pavement, moving toward Castle Street. This is, true to its name, a street dominated by a castle. Booth bought Hay Castle in 1971 for £10,000, and it is probably worth a million today, even with half its structure now gutted by fire. On the street below the castle is a row of old shops, some with the same owners for generations – the watchmaker, the greengrocer just a step below street level, the H. R. Grant & Son newsagent. A few townspeople, and a couple of visitors – known around here as book tourists – are poking about the storefronts, or fumbling with their cards at an ATM machine.

Directly across from the castle is Hay Booksellers, a store crammed into a sagging Tudor and filled with pleasant old books on one side and remaindered new books on the other. A woman working the counter and a local man, who I take to be another bookseller, are chatting when I walk in. They hardly notice me, so I bury my face in an 1829 copy of *Arcana of Science*:

Faculties of Brutes. The dog is the only animal that dreams; and he and the elephant are the only animals that understand looks; the elephant is the only animal that, besides man, feels ennui; the dog, the only quadruped that has been brought to speak. Leibnitz bears witness to a hound in Saxony, that could speak distinctly thirty words.

But I can't help listening to words being spoken at the counter instead.

"This Internet, I don't know what good it is."

"No good t'all. Nobody makes money on it."

"Customers can't see the book. Condition's everything in a used book."

"That's right. They can't pick it up and look at it, feel it." The man nods sagely. "So, what's the use?"

I am tempted to interrupt, to correct them, and then I decide: no, let it rest. I buy antiquarian books online all the time; for a scholar who depends on old books, it is a wondrous tool. And people do make money from it. But when you search online, you generally already know what it is that you are looking for. To look for a specific book in Hay is a hopeless task; you can only find the books that are looking for you, the ones you didn't even know to ask for in the first place. You come to Hay so that you can pick up a magazine you've never even heard of and read about Leibnitz's talking hound.

I like filthy old books. No, not that kind: though I've seen a few of those too. I mean the kind where the bindings are falling apart, the ones with what bookbinders call *red rot* – where, rather than properly tanning calfskin with oak bark, the publisher used cheap goatskin and just tossed a vial of acid in at the tannery, then didn't wash it properly afterward. It's always the most ephemeral books that suffered from this slapdash binding, the books never meant to last, and those are the books that I like best. After you handle them, they leave your hands and the front of your shirt covered in reddish brown smudges.

After browsing through old almanacs and bound issues of *Cornhill Magazine* piled on the store's staircase, I can feel the leather dust accumulating on the back of my throat. It is time for soda.

The nearest place is up the street at the Spar Market, where travelers are well advised to learn this trick: drink your soda while keeping your mouth shut. For while Hay does not have a public address system, it does have its grocers, newsagents, and publicans, and they seem to perform the same duty. There is not much privacy in this little or any other British village anyway, but that is not because Hay is little or a village. It is because it's British. You can immerse yourself in the media for months here and never hear the phrase *right to privacy*. The British have no particular opposition to such a right; they just never think to ask for it in the first place. There is no constitutional basis for privacy in this country; except for the government's privacy, that is. The Criminal Procedure and Investigations Act allows the crown to effectively withhold evidence from defense lawyers, and government misdeeds scurry beneath the rock of the Official Secrets Act.

Her Majesty's subjects have always lived with rather unseemly spying. The June 29, 1844, issue of *The Illustrated London News* includes a front-page article simply titled "The Secret Office, General Post Office." The Secret Office, operating under the approval of the home secretary, shared quarters with the GPO's money order department, and the newspaper engraving shows two rows of determined-looking young men seated at a long table, diligently opening the citizenry's mail:

Few persons are aware of how letters are opened and re-sealed by the Post Office. Wafers are opened by the application of moisture, and sealed letters are opened thus: – The letter is laid on an anvil with the seal up, upon the seal is laid a square piece of pure lead, and upon this lead descends a hammer with considerable velocity. The sudden impact converts the lead into [the mold of] a seal as faithful as an electrotype, and accordingly is used to re-seal the letter . . . In small country-towns, curious postmistresses keep by them an assortment of seals, with impressions of hearts, darts, etc., for the purpose of allowing them to get at little secrets.

The current home secretary and his minions would do their prying predecessors proud; Britain was an early and enthusiastic adopter of a shadowy network for monitoring calls and e-mails made by its citizens. And it is surely a marvelous system. Why, just this week IRA members set up a rocket launcher in a park across from the MI6 building in London, adjusted the launcher until it was just right, and then lobbed a missile into the superduper top-secret spymaster offices; probably as Her Majesty's finest were busy intercepting an e-mail containing a recipe for caramel flan.

"Afternoon," the woman at the Spar counter says. A customer turns to observe me.

"Afternoon," I confirm.

It is easy to find soda in the Spar, for the cramped little market is top-heavy with sugar in all its forms. Even alleged fruit juice invariably turns out, upon inspection, to be a fruit drink with perhaps 10 per cent juice. The rest is sweetener, a much beloved addition, for Britain has the world's highest per capita sugar consumption. How sweet is the British tooth? Well, they use sugar and aspartame and saccharin here – all in the same drink. Even their Sweet'n Low has aspartame, so that if you are deathly allergic to the stuff, you will die facedown in your cup of Earl Grey. But they have national health, so your next of kin won't get a big medical bill.

Jennifer is allergic to aspartame; she becomes short of breath. I am the queen's taster, so to speak, constantly dashing bottled British drinks out of her hands. "Look" – I will point at the label – *"aspartame."*

I set my bottle next to the cash register.

"Ninety-five pence."

I lay my gold-colored pound coin on the counter with a pleasing click, and the clerk hands me back a flimsy 5p piece. There is something deeply satisfying in Britain's use of coinage as its base unit of currency: paper money has an unreal quality of make-believe, as it is a symbolic medium that constantly reminds you of its arbitrary significance; for all you know, they could be printing it out by the gazillions up in cloud-cuckoo land. But coins are cold and hard and real. When you slap down pound coins on a wooden pub bar, then you, my friend, are *drinking*.

I take the long way around back to Lion Street; this involves crossing a precarious blind intersection at the end of Castle Street, and rounding the old Clock Tower. There is, by this intersection, a sign pointing to Merlin's Walk, a suspiciously new-sounding name. It was probably called something like the Sheep Trail, if it even had a name at all. But those who cannot make meaning out of the world given to them will invoke an ancient one and appropriate ill-understood past myths when convenient: Arthurian knights, druids, Indians, Egyptians, it hardly matters which. If any modern druids encountered genuine ancient ones out on the moors, the pretenders would probably be found the next morning with their throats slit. Imagine someone a few thousand years from now flailing around a censer, hooting some random Latin, and then yelling, *"Look at me, I'm a Catholic!"*

I pause in front of Booth's; I am ready.

The interior forcefully reminds you that it was not always a bookstore. It is both massive and massively constructed, with thick beams and floorboards designed to hold up heavy cast-iron factory machinery. Once it engineered agriculture implements, and now it supports a store of books on, among other topics, engineering and agriculture.

Not long after setting up shop in Hay, Booth vowed to make it the bookselling capital of the world, a pledge that was met with great hilarity. But one by one in the late sixties and early seventies, the local cinema, firehouse, castle, and factories were filled with books; Booth was buying them at pennies on the dollar in the United States as old seminaries went bankrupt, as ignoramuses staffing Peabody Libraries sold off their treasures – because "nobody reads them" – as New York literary institutions like Stechert Hafner shut their doors, and as little old rich ladies died and left libraries to half-literate progeny. These hauls were brought over on container ships and dumped out in countryside barns and slowly sorted by long-suffering employees, who in turn defected to found their own bookstores down the street.

It is now easier to find most works of American literature out in the Welsh countryside than it is to find them anywhere in America itself. Readers like me make yearly pilgrimages to Hay; the sheer weight of so many books has created its own gravitational pull, and we are caught in its orbit. And it is its own little kingdom: on April Fools' Day in 1977, Booth held a press conference in his castle to announce that Hay was now its own principality, that he was its king, and that it was going to start issuing passports. It didn't exactly turn into *Passport to Pimlico,* but no matter; now everybody knows where Hay-on-Wye is, and Booth is eternally its king.

Two employees have knives out and are zipping open newly arrived boxes when I walk into Booth's; I can only pick out disjointed words from their conversation as I pass:

"It will get to be a crisis with these books . . ."

". . . storage . . ."

". . . shipment . . ."

". . . arrival tomorrow . . ."

I wander back through crowded shelves of nature books – look at all these beautiful old copies of *Pepacton*! – and through shelfloads of bound *National Geographic*s to make my way toward the back barn, a hidden annex that I never even noticed until my third trip to Hay. Passing through a room of musty old science fiction paperbacks, I see a magazine discarded on a dirty concrete stairway – *Popular Science Monthly*. It is not even priced. It is the December 1878 issue:

> Professor Fischer, who was lately found dead in the laboratory of the Prague Gymnasium, was the victim of a theory. Having mixed sal-ammoniac with cyanide of potassium, he bade his attendant to note how "science has advanced so far as even to be able to render harmless so dangerous an agent as cyanide of potassium." With this he tasted the mixture, was quickly seized with violent pains, and expired before a physician could arrive . . .

And so forth. I blow a layer of fine grit off the cover, tuck the magazine under my arm, and press onward.

Once I'm inside the barn hidden out back, I notice a side room. I've not seen it in the past, never even noticed a door there before. Have you had this dream? A dream of another room in your house, one you'd somehow not perceived in your years of living there, by some wondrously strange blind spot – and so you grasp the cool metal knob and turn it, and it turns easily, and the door slowly creaks open, and inside there is light, there is confusion . . .

I walk in.

It is appalling. Books are stacked everywhere in toppled and crumbling piles. Here, nineteenth-century physics books in German, printed in unmistakable thick Teutonic black letter. There, a 1974 issue of *Mad* magazine, featuring a TV parody titled, of course,

"McClod." Over here, an early edition of Tennyson. Underneath that, *Aunt Judy's Christmas Annual 1876.*

I look at the books: still no prices. It dawns on me that perhaps I'm not supposed to be here. But I hear someone coming, and so I piously bury myself in the contents page of the Tennyson volume. A man's labored breathing comes nearer.

It is an employee. He is shelving a few books – a hopeless task! Each time the aged man leans forward to pick nuggets off this mountain of print, he lets off a wheeze and a groan. Books are hard work; and clearly this fellow has enough hard work even without the books.

He has not seen me in here. But I finally set Tennyson down and reach for another volume – some dreadful missionary text.

He looks up at me. "This is a storage area," he apologizes. "But look around, if you like."

Half his face is frozen, and his voice slurred, presumably from a stroke; his eyes swim in thick corrective lenses.

"Oh, sorry," I stutter. "I didn't realize. But thank you."

"Do I detect an American accent?"

"San Francisco."

"Ah! I've been there. Quite nice."

"Oh, I love it. Though actually, I've just moved over here."

"What, to England?"

"No, Hay."

His eyebrows rise up and he guffaws. "What an extraordinary choice. What brought you here?"

"I . . ." And for a moment, I really don't know. "It just seemed like the right place to be."

"Mmm."

"I write," I blurt out. "About eighteenth- and nineteenth-century literature. Especially obscure literature. And this just seemed the perfect place to do that. Also, I've got a little boy, and . . . well, I thought a childhood in the country might be good for him."

"That I do understand," he says plainly. "It's lovely here." He sorts and shelves a few more books. "So you know American literature?"

"Um . . . well, I guess . . ."

"Come with me."

I follow him back into the recesses of the building, where the American lit is shelved and stacked haphazardly. My best finds are here; on a previous trip I'd found a first edition of *Mercy Philbrick's Choice,* an extraordinary fictional portrayal of artistic isolation that Emily Dickinson's friend Helen Hunt Jackson published while the poet was still alive, and still unknown. In reading a description of the character of Mercy, thousands of readers unwittingly had the idea of an Emily Dickinson before they ever heard of the actual woman:

> There is the making of a glorious woman and, I think, a true poet in this girl; but whether she makes either will depend entirely upon the hands she falls into . . . She would contentedly make bread and do nothing else, till the day of her death, if that seemed to be the nearest and most demanded duty . . . I am often distressed by her lack of impulse worship. I think she has no strong sense of a personal God; yet her conscience is in many ways morbidly sensitive.

Jackson even wrote Dickinson to ask for help with the book, to publish some poems, anything – "I have a little manuscript volume with a few of your verses in it – and I read them very often – You are a great poet – and it is a wrong to the day you live in, that you will not sing aloud," Jackson scolded. *"When you are what men call dead, you will be sorry you were so stingy."* The author was nearly as well hidden as her subject: the book was published by Thomas Niles to inaugurate his No Name Series, which published new works by writers like Jackson, Louisa May Alcott, and Christina Rossetti anonymously, allowing the works to stand or fall in review columns on their own merits. It is hard to imagine hype-hungry publishers undertaking such a project today.

"For a book town to survive" – the man coughs – "you need specialists. *Eh-brugh-ugh! [Ugh.]* And American literature – well, it *is* the superpower. We're a declining country . . ." He trails off. "You know, there is more of a market for old American books here than in America itself. But right now" – he gestures to the stacks – "It's chaos. Just chaos."

He pauses and turns to me. "Will you meet me tomorrow for lunch?"

"Uh" – I am startled – "I guess. Sure. Where?"

"I'll be in the castle, in the kitchen."

I've never eaten in a castle before – not even a ruined one. The only notion I have of living in such a place comes from reading *I Capture the Castle.*

"Okay. What time?"

"Be there at quarter to one."

He departs with a clutch of ancient books and pauses in the doorway.

"By the way," he adds, almost as an afterthought. "My name is Richard Booth. And this is my bookshop."

Chapter Six
Vegetates in Front of the Telly

"I FOUND AN apartment for us to rent," Jennifer says when I get back. "Look." She passes me a pamphlet from the town's tourist office, with a circled listing —

SIXTEENTH CENTURY APARTMENT.

"That sounds fun."

"I talked to the woman who owns it. She runs Pemberton's bookshop" – virtually the only seller of new books, God forbid, in this town – "and the apartment is on top of the bookstore. It looks right out over the old Butter Market."

"I've always wanted to live in a bookstore."

"Well, now you can. She said we can move in tonight." Jennifer turns her completed jigsaw puzzle to face me. "An alpine meadow," she sighs. "Get a good look at it, because I'm about to knock it to pieces."

We spend the afternoon repacking and watching the telly. No matter what any guidebook tells you, this is the best way to spend your time in Britain. UK television is not intrinsically better than American – it has just as much dreck, especially the hilariously atrocious soaps they import from Australia, the writers of which should probably be thrown from the top of the Sydney Opera House. But there are also shows here that are vastly smarter than any U.S. programming. They assume a level of intelligence and specialized interest that no U.S. program would dare to, *even if that intelligence and interest does not actually exist* – because when there are only six broadcast channels, you can be certain that a fair portion of the population will watch it anyway. The BBC operates in blissful disregard of ratings. At eight P.M. tonight on the Beeb? A documentary on "our industrial heritage" in which "our host searches the country for a beam-engine." The other channel has, I think, a *snooker tournament*.

Even their game shows are smarter here. My favorite is *Count-down,* which could advertise itself in the following manner:

Are you . . .

An unemployed grad student?
An overeducated homemaker?
A retired bank clerk?
Autistic?

If so, then you have probably already been a contestant on Countdown. *You needn't read any further.*

The first show ever broadcast on Channel 4, *Countdown* is now a staple of playwright-on-the-dole afternoon viewing. It's a quiz show based around potential anagrams: you pick nine random letters from stacks of consonants and vowels, and then you have thirty seconds to string together the longest word you can think of. Like any good British invention, it was actually nicked from the French and then greatly improved upon.

What *Countdown* lacks, though, is prize money. British game shows have always been strangely parsimonious. Because for years they were only broadcast on nationalized television, it meant that they were government supported, and it might have been unseemly to give thousands of pounds in taxpayer funds to someone simply because they can anagram IDLEFOUR into FLUORIDE – though I suppose the MI6 often does just that. And so for years British game shows got away with prizes that would make a midway carny look generous – egg timers, frosted drinking glasses, and the like. One show was known for chasing down contestants in the parking lot to force them to take their "prizes" with them, since the lucky winners were prone to abandon them behind the stage curtain and under cushions in the greenroom.

Even as lucre – piles of it, potentially – begins to infiltrate the game shows here, this quality lingers on. For the show that comes on next today is *15 to 1,* offering no daily prize at all. Yet the grand prize at the end of this year is stunning. It is actual Greek pottery, a bowl illustrated with naked figures, from 400 B.C. – a really beautiful piece, something that would normally belong in a museum. This is the prize that some bus driver from Norwich will be taking home and placing next to the ceramic kittens on his mantel.

Can you imagine, in America, giving away anything used on a game show – a furnishing not made by Broyhill or La-Z-Boy or Ethan Allen? To give away an old bowl that was once covered with *dirt?* Why, your contestants would pull out their licensed concealed handguns and plug you one in the gut.

It gets stranger still. Today, finding himself with some extra time to kill, because the contestants have been bumped off so quickly, the *15 to 1* host – a teacherly fellow named William Stewart – begins to lecture his audience on *why the Elgin Marbles should be returned to Greece*.

Stop a moment to think upon this.

The British game-show host must first assume that his audience knows what the Elgin Marbles are, and that they even care. Or, for that matter, that they know where *Greece* is. You are not allowed to do any of these things with the chimp's tea party that is an American audience, as it might interfere with their swinging their forearms about and yelling *hoo-hoo-hoo-hoo-HOO!*

The only U.S. game-show host to use his massive national exposure to espouse anything remotely controversial is the aptly named Bob Barker – though standing up for cuddly animals is not exactly risking public censure. But here is Mr. Stewart taking up a position in defiance of the government, the Foreign Office, the British Museum – in defiance of the old notion of Britishness, even – and saying we should give the Greeks back their ancient statues, and if their incompetent curators want to ruin them, then by god that is their right. Can you imagine a U.S. game-show host, on the air, taking issue with U.S. foreign policy? With the fine points of antiquities treaties? The notion is simply beyond the range of thinkable thoughts.

A nastier side of British life can also be glimpsed in their game shows. We watch *The Weakest Link* in the United States to see contestants sass back at the host – but the British version is, if one can imagine, altogether more unpleasant, for their contestants do not talk back. When a woman in a suit tells Brits that they are worthless, they hang their heads in shame. They *agree* with her. How else can one explain Thatcher's decade in office? That said, even Anne Robinson can go too far. Sniping at one contestant "Do you cut your own hair?" generated complaints; for Ms. Robinson's not particularly subtle implication transgressed this nation's fundamental Law of the Classes: you do not humiliate the poor to their face. It is acceptable to shut them out of your clubs and your governance, but only by alluding to their *unfitness* for the task. The matter of money is not to be mentioned.

It is, however, acceptable to gripe about the rich. And this too begins to be revealed as money flows into their game shows. When their *Who Wants to Be a Millionaire?* finally had a million-pound winner, newspapers looked through the society registers and then pounced: the winner was *already* wealthy, they announced. How dare she win another million pounds? And here is their difference from us. First, no American would bother to find out the assets of a quiz show or lottery winner. And while there is class resentment in America, the poor do not take it to a personal level: they vent at the mayor, at the police, at local businesses, at other poor people, at everyone but the rich themselves – because they want to be rich too, and would do the same. If you have a million and win another million, Americans will not spit at you.

They will say, "Wow. Now you have *two* million."

We trundle into Pemberton's loaded down with a stroller and but a few of our many bags, staggering clumsily; Jennifer bashes over a display of local authors as we enter, and I in turn nearly amputate the cover from a copy of *Kilvert's Diary*.

"Can I help you?" the clerk asks.

"Yes." Our bags thud to the floor. "Is, um" – rustling of papers – *"Diana Blunt* here?"

"She's down in the storeroom. Will you be renting upstairs?"

"Yes, that's us."

"Wonderful!" The clerk disappears down a staircase, leaving us alone in the store.

Pemberton's is a curious little store, for it is an independent seller of new books: a rare breed in the States, and rarer still in any part of the UK outside Charing Cross. Book chains have ruled this country for so long that the fact hardly elicits any notice. No one can much remember a time before Waterstone's, WH Smith, and Blackwell's. And before them, it was Boots – a catchall drugstore today, it built up a bookselling and book-lending empire in the 1800s by leaping early at railway distribution and profiting nicely from rather nasty pieces of work like the *Awful Disclosures* by Maria Monk. That was an 1836 exposé of a Montreal convent where priests impregnated nuns, strangled the resulting infants, and then tossed the little unfortunates into a lime-filled pit under the convent. Monk's fame did not last: visiting teams of investigators found that the interior of the convent did not quite match the book's description – as in, there were no secret tunnels, satanic ritual rooms, infant-bone piles, or steaming cauldrons presided over by the Weird Sisters – and Monk was awarded a permanent writer's residency in a New York prison after she was caught pickpocketing.

I poke around the store a little more. Pemberton's is not large, though it is efficiently packed. But I start to notice a pattern: certain bestsellers are altogether missing, while other writers – Margaret Atwood, say, or Bruce Chatwin – are represented in abundance. The longer you look at the shelves, the more you suspect that what you are looking at is a sort of personal library, a living room with a cash register. There is a person behind the selection here, guiding you with a not-quite-invisible hand.

"Are you Jennifer and Paul? And Morgan?" a voice calls out from downstairs.

"Yes, hello!"

"I'll be up in a minute – I must find the keys."

The clerk comes back up and stands aside, for following her is Diana, the store's owner. If Mr. Booth is the king of Hay, then Mrs. Blunt may be its undeclared queen, though she is quite the opposite from him: where he is rumpled, stricken, and hidden under prescription glass, she is striking, poised, and perhaps a little intimidating.

"I'm Diana, and this is my assistant Hazel. These are your keys. One is for the courtyard door, which is locked at six, and the other is for your apartment – you're on the top floor, and your entranceway is left of the accountant's office."

I fumble the keys into my pocket.

"You're not sure yet how long you'll be in Hay?" she adds.

"Permanently, I hope."

"Oh?"

"We're moving to Hay," Jennifer explains. "We'll be househunting."

"Really? Have you looked out in Warren Close?"

"Um. Yes."

"There are quite reasonable houses out there."

"Yes. There are."

Diana does not seem like the kind of person you disagree with. Before we trudge upstairs, I buy a book from her, off the local-author shelf that we nearly wrecked. It is *The Book of Hay,* by Kate Clarke; so titled because the words *Hay* and *book* can never be very far apart anymore.

The building has been here for ever, it seems; its mailing address within Hay is, quite simply, The Apartment, 4 High Town. It is reached by back courtyard stairs, which take us past each of Diana's other tenants – a furniture restorer, an Eastern European bookseller, and an accountant. So half of the building's occupants sell books, which is about par for Hay-on-Wye.

We drag our bags up and unlock our door, to reveal yet two more flights of stairs. I bound up the stairs in one last burst of energy and immediately knock my skull on a hard piece of wood. The doorways in these old homes are about five feet ten inches high; if you are six feet tall, much bone-cracking merriment will ensue.

The Apartment takes up the top two floors of the building, which must be one of the largest in the town's center. It is perfect: creaking wood, beams everywhere, and it looks out commandingly over the town below. The top floor is two bedrooms, which arch in with the roof, all heavy beams and big wooden pegs, and an assortment of exceedingly solid joists and bars and nuts and massy bolts. A shipbuilder might be able to figure out what actually holds it all together, since the ceiling looks exactly as if someone flipped the keel of an old clipper ship upside down. And maybe they did: I once worked at a friend's ad shop on Jackson Street in San Francisco, and the timbers of that building were scavenged from ships scuttled in the San Francisco Bay. Some of that city's downtown was built over a breakwater constructed of these ships; every time they dig a new tunnel there, they hit an old copper-sheathed hull.

After dragging the rest of the bags over from the Seven Stars, I settle into The Apartment's downstairs living room, rub the collection of beam-shaped bruises on my forehead, and leaf through the pamphlets jammed into a bookcase. Wookey Hole! Legoland! The coal pits of Wales!

I sigh and pick up my newly bought *Book of Hay*.

"Hey," I yell to the kitchen. "This place is in the book."

"What place?"

"This one – The Apartment. Says here it was a meetinghouse. A secret one, for Quakers, back when they were outlawed."

Why, the building is probably riddled with priest's holes and hidden compartments – Maria Monk would be so jealous – if only I knew which wall panel to lean on, which statue to poke the eyes of! Surely a claw hammer and a crowbar could reveal a great deal, though I don't suppose Diana would appreciate my enthusiasm for demolishing her walls. But you never know: why, just last year, builders in Cornwall found a severed hand inside a wall. They think it may have been blown off when a stray German bomb hit a cottage, whereupon the unlucky fist migrated with great velocity into some setting concrete.

But I am whistling past the graveyard – or past the physical therapist's office, at any rate. Writers tend to feel a little vulnerable about their hands and fingers, the most basic tools of the trade. I still cannot bring myself to use a kitchen sink garbage disposal; even with the power shut off, it's the thought of those whirring blades, under that slick wet rubber aperture that you must sometimes stick your fingers through: I cannot stand it. It's a fear doubled by my being a musician; I know of one guitarist who will not shake hands with anyone for fear that they will break his long and delicate fingers. My fingers are not his, exactly: mine have fat little callused pads at the end, fit only for bass guitar. But no matter; I still avoid all contact sports and will not reach my hand into anything that I cannot see inside of. My fingers look easily broken to *me,* if not to anyone else.

I am not the only one to be convinced of this hidden fragility. I was lucky to find at Booth's a copy of Dr. William Hammond's 1883 book, *A Treatise on Insanity in Its Medical Relations*. Hammond is a medical hero of mine, if for no other reason than that, while working as a Union army doctor during the Civil War, he cured a soldier of "the belief that he was inhabited by chicken bones." Later on, in private practice, Hammond encountered all sorts of strange patients: a woman who hallucinated Grecian masks leering out at her from around street corners and from behind store shelves; a man who would only take orders whispered to him by a ticking clock on his mantel; a plumber who received messages from "The Boss Plumber of Eternity," informing him that a combination of shark blood and shark urine would create an unbreakable steam-pipe solder. But one case of a man desperately protecting his frail hand is what stays in my mind:

> The delusions of the intellectual monomaniac may relate to changes which he supposes have taken place in various parts of his body. A gentleman conceived that his right hand was made of glass, and therefore kept it carefully enclosed in a stout case, made to fit it accurately. On my calling his attention to the physical qualities of his hand, and pointing out how they differed from those of glass, he said: "I once thought just as you do. My hand looks like flesh and blood, but it is glass for all that. Nothing is more calculated to deceive the senses."

It hardly mattered that the man was intelligent and perceptive in every other way. "While able to perceive the ludicrous character of the delusions of their fellow-lunatics, they cling tenaciously to their own, which are perhaps more ridiculous," Hammond explains . . .

(Ah, but couldn't that be said of all of us?)

". . . *Look at that poor woman,* said a gentleman to me as we walked through the grounds of an asylum; *she has lost her baby, and she thinks she has it in that bundle of rags she is nursing.* Yet he was himself under the delusion that he was General Grant."

Oh. Perhaps *that* couldn't be said of all of us.

And yet there is something strangely compelling in that notion that our bodies are as frail as glass containers. A whole book was once written around this conceit: Elinor Wylie's 1925 fable, *The Venetian Glass Nephew.* It is set in the Renaissance, and in it, an archbishop ardently wishes for a child to call his own. An obliging sculptor makes him a living and breathing child . . . of glass. Inevitably, the child grows up and longs to belong to and find love in a world of flesh and hard, shattering edges. But he can never fit in, of course; and when he shakes hands with people, they find tiny glass splinters in their palms afterward.

Of course, this whole glass allegory can also be rendered rather less . . . well, poetical. There used to be a lovely literary freak show here in Britain called *The Wonderful Magazine*. Or rather, it was more fully called *The Wonderful Magazine, and Marvelous Chronicle of Extraordinary Productions, Events, and Occurrences, in Nature and Art: Consisting Entirely of Matter Which Come Under the Denomination of MIRACULOUS! QUEER! ODD! STRANGE! SUPERNATURAL! WHIMSICAL! ABSURD! OUT OF THE WAY! And UNACCOUNTABLE!* It is full of tales of men taking bets to see how long they can roast themselves in a bread oven, of petrified toads found in calciferous springs, and so forth. After one story of an artist "who verily believed that all the bones of his body were to become so flexible and soft, that they might easily be crushed together, and folded one within the other, as a piece of wax," there comes another account delivered with a straight face: "There was one who thought his posteriors were made of glass; so that all he did he performed standing; fearing, that if he should sit down, he should break his bottom."

An excellent argument for overstuffed chairs. But the *Wonderful Magazine* then adds:

> Montanus tells of one who thought all the [surface] of the world was made of thin and transparent glass, and that underneath there lay a multitude of serpents; that he lay in his bed as in an island, whence if he should presume to venture, that then he should break the glass, and so falling amongst the serpents, he should speedily be devoured; and therefore, to prevent that misfortune, he was resolved never to stir from his bed.

A disturbing notion, isn't it? – and a good reason to go to bed and stay in it.

I wake up during the night. A man on the street below is talking, if that is the word. And, if I am to trust my ears, he seems to be gargling without the benefit of a sink. Ah! If vomiting could have a lilt, then I do believe that this vomiting does.

The man is saying —

"Bluurrgh-ga-gahg. *Jaysus.*"

Then he adds —

"Bluurrgh-ga-gahg. *Jaysus.*"

And further observes —

"Bluurrgh-ga-gahg. *Jaysus.*"

I do not bother to roll over to check the clock; there is no need. I know already that it is surely six minutes after closing time; and that we are seventy steps from a pub door.

When I fully wake up, it is to sunlight and the sound of sober voices, distant sounds blurred together by our distance from the ground. It sounds like a streetful of Wallaces and Gromits.

"What's going on out there?" Jennifer says from the bed as Morgan nurses, and I stick my head out a window.

"Market Day."

Our bedroom window overlooks the Butter Market, a stone-columned, covered market from the town's early-Victorian heyday.

It is late in the morning, and I am too tired and lazy to buy any food down there, so I rifle through the food that previous guests have left in our kitchen. Marmite, a full box of PG Tips, a tin of curry powder, sugar cubes, plump white cartons of UHT milk; I finally settle upon Weetabix – this is a sort of shredded doormat – and munch vacantly while reading through the book I found yesterday at Booth's. *Health and Beauty: How Obtained,* by Shirley Dare. She was, from what I can tell, a syndicated beauty columnist in Baltimore during the 1890s. I highly recommend perusing her responses to reader letters:

E. says: "I have been taking arsenical wafers since March, and they have done me no good; so, if you will, tell me something to cure pimples quick; I don't care what it is."

Try first this wash: one-half ounce of powdered borax, one ounce glycerine, one pint camphor water; mix and wet the face with it twice a day, leaving it to dry on, then wash off in soft water. If after using a fortnight no relief is found, wash the face with a strong soft soap at night and apply powdered sulphur wet with spirits of camphor. Let the paste stay on all night; wash off next morning, and rub face with cerate.

Nina wants to know the quickest way of making the hands and wrists plump.

Soak them in a bowl of hot olive oil before sleeping, and wear loose castor gloves all night. In the middle of the day, rub hand and wrists briskly ten minutes, first one hand a moment, then the other, then rub well with warm perfumed oil. Soaking the hands in warm milk also nourishes and whitens them.

A Reader asks: "What shall I do to make my face plump? I weigh 135, but look as if I did not weigh over 120. I eat a great

deal of oatmeal, etc., but it doesn't seem to make any difference."

The treatment of such cases by the schools of physical culture is to rub and work the lower parts of the cheeks ten to twenty times each half-day. Rubbing them with almond oil or toilet cerate at night restores plumpness, when used with exercise. Work the jaws up and down, as if eating, with the mouth shut, ten minutes at a time. Also, lift the chin as high as possible and drop it 100 times at each exercise. This treatment should be kept up three months to see any marked change.

I do laugh at Miss Dare. How can I not? But it is the laughter, I think, of recognition.

Because I write history, I am often asked this question: If I could live in any year, what year would I choose? This is a question I can always answer without hesitation: I would like to live *next year,* because then my book will be done and I will have my advance in hand.

Granted, I live a life filled with the past. And yet I could not live in the past, because I could not *live* in the past. The past is dead to me because I am dead to it: dead in a premature birth, dead on a fence spike that speared my left temple at the age of three, dead of a collapsed lung at eighteen, dead of pneumonia at twenty-nine. I am a dead, dead man. Without incubators and antibiotics, we are all mere notations in the town clerk's death records.

Even so, I will admit to a real fondness for the Victorians, because they amuse me. It's not just the Shirley Dares of the world that do this. They are all, you see, so like us in their hope and dread of technological progress, their goals of equality for women, their overarching ambitions for world culture and global markets, their miraculous tying together of continents in instant communication

. . . they are us. Here are people groping toward a universe of quantum mechanics, a world after Darwin, a country after monarchy, a sky and sea filled with mechanical contrivance. Their hopes and rhetoric are recognizably our own, but their tools are hilariously unequal to the task: they are future thinkers armed with nothing but leather, steel, stone, and porcelain. The friction between their dreams, which are recognizably ours, and their means, which are so quaint, is what makes the Victorians sympathetic and yet also absurd.

But then, I suppose every era looks a little foolish to its descendants. This is because the past is the only country where it is still acceptable to mock the natives. But we should not laugh too hard: for soon enough, we shall all live there.

Jennifer is mixing acrylics for a painting of Chinatown; scattered behind her are pages from *Bon-bon,* a novel she's writing about street kids in the Haight. Morgan is watching a *Sesame Street* video on TV, and on my side of the living room is a teetering pile of old American magazines from the 1800s that I found at Booth's. Somehow America looms larger to us now than when we actually lived there. We tune in to NPR online most nights and have a standing order each week at the newsagent for *The New Yorker* whenever it comes in, usually about two weeks out-of-date. Then we quietly swipe it back and forth from each other for the rest of the week. I suppose there may be a time when, bit by bit, Jennifer and I leave these relics behind, when America drifts away, to just another lumbering giant of a nation three thousand miles away from us and our thoughts.

I toss aside an old *Harper's* from 1871; it's minutes before twelve forty-five.

"Ah! Lunch!"

I kiss Morgan and Jennifer and then go clattering down our creaky staircase, pulling on a overshirt. I will have to sprint over to the castle. But there's no need; for once I get outside to the courtyard I find Richard Booth shuffling up High Town and in front of my gate.

"Hi."

He doesn't respond.

"Hi!" I repeat, louder.

Villagers pause; from one syllable, they know I am an American. Only Americans go around yelling *HI* at people in the street.

Richard looks up. "Ah, yes," he bellows. "Can you carry this for me?"

He gives me a plastic carrier bag loaded in equal parts with books and groceries. We walk up Castle Street, and he points up the hill at the tower looming before us.

"You've seen the castle before?"

"Just the bookshop portion."

"There was a fire, you know." He pauses to cough fitfully. "Some time back. Gutted the place, though we've got the ground floor together again."

The bare ruined windows, three and four stories up, stare out vacantly over the town, each framing blue sky behind them. This vacant stare, where the floors are gone and nothing but negative space is left inside the building walls and windows – I've seen it before. In Rhyolite, a Nevada ghost town of dynamited banks and hotels, where out of the rubble jutted up great slices of old buildings, empty shells, some with shreds of red curtains still high up in their top-story windows, flapping madly in the desert wind. But this place doesn't even have curtains.

We reach the top of some wooden stairs marked DANGER, and Richard calls to a staffer buried behind a nest of photography books.

"Could you let us in? The kitchen."

The fellow roots around and walks us to an oaken side door of the castle, producing from his pocket a skeleton key so weighty that he has clearly stolen it from Vincent Price. The door groans open with a sound like distant voices.

"I'll have to lock you in," the clerk says mournfully. "You can't get out."

The door creaks closed behind me, the lock closing with a *kerchunk*. As my eyes adjust to the dark, I see an old musket leaned against a wall, and neat stacks of old books.

"This way." Booth waves me forward.

I wander into a kitchen – sunlight filters in through the windows, and the floor is stone and cold. Carved devils grin down from corbels set against the ceiling beams.

"You," Booth tells me, *"are my new American."*

Blackwood's magazine, back when it was Poe's favorite source for inspiration, once ran a pleasant tale bearing the title "The Iron Shroud." In it, a prisoner locked in a dungeon comes to believe that, with each passing day, his cell is shrinking ever so slightly. So he strikes upon a cunning system of placing straws across the floor to prove it: the walls *were* closing in. Windows and entire sections of floor begin disappearing under the relentless and terrible progress of the stone walls. By the end, the despairing hero, Vivenzio, is left on his bed; as the walls bear down one last time, the bed frame twists and finally snaps in like a bear trap upon him.

The story is set in Sicily. But now the castle walls are closing in on me in Wales. I'm certain of it.

"Are you Jewish?" Booth blurts out.

"Hmm?" I look away from the stone corners of the room.

"Jewish? Are you?"

"Uh, no?"

"You won't object to a ham sandwich, then?"

"Not at all." Though, in truth, I don't like ham much.

He sets down a plastic bag on a counter by the sink.

"There's sandwiches in there," he says. "Help yourself."

I sit on a rough wooden bench, unwrap a sandwich, and munch on it. Booth takes out one for himself, finds a plate, and settles down heavily on a chair opposite me.

"You know about the quangoes here?" he demands.

"I thought they were extinct."

"Extinct?" he explodes in disbelief.

"The zebras?"

"Quangoes," he roars. "You are thinking of *quaggas*. I am talking about *quangoes*."

"Quangoes."

"Quasi-Autonomous Non-Governmental Organizations. The Milk Board, the Welsh Tourist Board, the Forestry Commission . . . all that lot." He waves a hand dismissively. "They call them nongovernmental, but they're propped up with tax money. To build luxury hotels in farming and coal towns, that sort of nonsense."

"Ah."

"The quangoes are *killing* Hay," he says flatly, and pauses to cough percussively. "A town needs a reason to live. And you won't find it in the Tourist Information Center. Or shops full of Welsh key chains and souvenir shotglasses, that kind of rubbish. This town's reason to live is *books*."

"I can see that."

"It used to be cider." He nods at my glass. "But now it is books."

"Hmm."

"So." He eyes me suddenly. "You're an expert on American literature?"

"Oh, I don't know if I'd – "

"We need experts like you," he barrels on. "We need an American, an American expert."

A figure materializes out from a corner passage – a woman, somewhat younger than Booth – and passes into the kitchen, snapping on the faucet.

"Hope, this is *Paul,*" Booth bellows across the room to her.

"Hello, Paul," she says, at a volume precisely inverse to Booth's. "I'm Hope."

She is making a cup of tea, and just from watching I feel she must be Booth's wife, and that this may not be the first time that she has walked in on a ham-sandwich lecture on quangoes and book experts.

"Yes, an American expert. You must understand, Paul," Booth slurs through his stroke a little, "it's not about the buying. From now on it has to be about selling."

He empties a clutch of books out of a plastic bag.

"Look at the bloody things." He pokes at them lifelessly. "Buying them is the easy part. Sid and I do it all the time. You go and knock on old ladies' doors and give them fifty quid for a roomful of books. *Trained monkeys* could do it. What we need is someone to decide where all these books go, how we can sell them and turn a profit."

Hope sits down across the table and regards me with a raised eyebrow.

"So what Paul will do," Booth explains to her between bites of his sandwich, "is work *anarchistically*. In the American literature section."

This, I feel, is an accurate prediction.

Chapter Seven
Pays Its Respects

"COME TO READING," my uncle Ivor tells me on the phone. "Quickly."

My grandmother Nan is eighty-three now, I think, and not faring well; she became increasingly irritable over the month of August – "It's the first time," my mother commented, "that I've ever heard her *whiny*." And then, one day, as she left her little council flat in Sonning-on-Thames, she was robbed – struck from behind by a heavy object, her frail little body crumpling to the ground.

Only she wasn't. A neighbor rushed over to her on the ground – where she was screaming, *Police, police, police, I've been attacked* – and sat her up.

— Nan, nobody's touched you. You just fell down.

— ? —

— There was no robber, Nan.

— ? —

And so forth. My uncle Ivor took her to the hospital, where she lost her mind – wailing, thrashing about in her bed, and pulverizing her brittle arms black and blue with bruises, screaming nightmares – until the drugs finally kicked in.

The doctor took my uncle aside to tell him of his mother: she will die.

Brain cancer. She is an eighty-three-year-old woman with brain cancer. And when you are an eighty-three-year-old woman with brain cancer in Great Britain, you will die at the age of eighty-three. Of brain cancer. Heroic measures are not taken here; they save that for people who still have their lives ahead of them.

And there's more, he said: she has lung cancer too.

"How's his temperature?"

I am gripping the phone so hard that it will melt. "Thirty-eight point five . . ." Damn, damn, *damn* these Celsius thermometers. I am frantically performing fractions in my head. "Which is, uh, one hundred and one point five?"

The nurse on the phone is soothing: keep your baby hydrated, keep him uncovered, give him infant paracetamol, watch for vomiting or rashes or distress. If his temperature goes higher, bring him in.

We are in a tatty hotel room in Reading, and Jennifer is nursing our sick baby to sleep. We want Nan to see her great-grandson once, before she dies, but now he's the one that we're all worried about. He was suddenly hit by diarrhea on the train over, and he's roasting himself internally. Instead of hooting and pouncing on us in the train, Morgan just . . . stopped. He cuddled up, whimpered a little, and made his yoodling noises ever so quietly. It was adorable until we figured out why: he was scared and exhausted.

He is looking up at his mother and then me as he nurses.

"Oh, sweetie." I stroke his head.

"You should go," Jennifer says. "If Nan dies tonight, and you haven't seen her, you'll feel terrible."

"Yeah, but – Morgan."

"If I have to take Morgan to the doctor, I'll call, I'll leave you a note."

I know she is right. *Squick squick,* goes Morgan's sad little mouth.

I have never been alone in a room with my grandmother before. This strange fact dawns on me as I ride in the taxi to Nan's hospital. When I was a kid, I'd visit Cutbush, the mansion where she and my late grandfather Edwin lived – in dank servants' quarters, he being the gardener – but I'd always go with my uncle Richard and his kids. My cousins and I would root through the money bags in the barn, which were actually canvas sacks of bottle caps left behind by some long-gone theatrical troupe, and we'd chase each other around the maze of an English garden, alternating between yelping at nettle stings and frantically tearing every dock leaf in sight, rubbing them over our rashed bodies until we all smelled like sod. Nan always stayed inside with her flatulent little dog, and she would have cups of tea waiting for us when we came in; my grandfather would sometimes come outside to point out his tree grafts, or a good beehive to get stung at, or the property's old Roman gravestone – which, now that I think upon it, was suspiciously well preserved after two millennia.

It's already dark outside when the taxi drops me off in front of the Royal Berkshire Hospital. It is a massive Georgian edifice, all neoclassical columns and tanned sandstone, and it looks more like a place for handing out medals than for administering sponge baths. I walk inside; the lobby is empty – no staff, no nothing. The lights are buzzing overhead, and the place is dead quiet. No PA system is muttering for a doctor, nobody is racing through with gurneys. There is nothing but a linoleumed hallway stretching out into the distance, fluorescent light pooled in its plastic finish, and so I start walking.

I have not been in a hospital since Morgan was born. And yet – an ocean away, even – the feel is the same. The same swabbed floors, painted cinderblock walls, the same vending machines where wrung-out family members go in the middle of the night for some morsel, even if just sugar, to sustain them a little longer.

It is visiting hour, and yet since arriving, I have not seen a single other human being. Finally, a sign for the Nuffield unit. I follow it past a nurses' station and into a ward filled with gowned bodies, ailing women stretched out on metal beds.

And then – I think? – I see her.

"Nan?"

She looks up. "Oh! Oh! You've come!" she bursts, and claps. And now I know it is my grandmother, because I know the voice – and, yes, now I see the face. But she is different now. She has lost weight, and angry purple bruises spill across her arms and legs. But most of all, her hair has gone absolutely white.

We talk, I don't even know about what. I am smiling like a dummy the whole time, trying to be cheery, all along thinking, oh my God, she's going to die. But she is happy that we are moving out to the country, and that Morgan will grow up out there.

"A childhood in the country, that's something you can never get back when you're grown up," she says. "Don't matter how much money you have, do it? You couldn't get me to live in town."

She stops to put on her sunglasses. The light hurts her eyes, and these are prescription sunglasses – she's lost her regular pair, and now these are the only way that she can see the time pass on the wall clock at the other side of the ward. It being nighttime, the only light reflected off them comes from the ceiling fixtures.

"You know, when your father" – she's confused and is now actually talking of my uncle Ivor – "when your father was little, in the countryside at Cutbush, I'd take him down to the paddock to see the cows. And one day, I imagine he was four, we went and there was a calf nursing at his mother. And your father saw that and he said, *Look, Mummy, that cow's eating sausages.*" She breaks out laughing. "What kids make of things, you just never know, do you?"

"I wonder if he remembers the cows now."

"I shouldn't think so. It was . . . so long ago."

I look around the ward. This ceiling, this green cinderblock wall – this is the last image on the eye. Before they slip away to . . .

. . . to . . .

"Sometimes I wonder," I tell her, "what Morgan's first memory will be."

"The countryside, I should think. The fresh air."

"That's what I'm hoping."

"Oh, but the countryside's not what it used to be. It's all changing."

"That's true," I agree. "There's already a lot happening around Hay. But then ag – " And I am about to say, but it depends on where you are, because in other places like France and New England, the rural land's becoming depopulated, and the forests are thicker than they were two hundred years ago – but she only hears the first part of what I've said.

"Yes, yes," she says, "the countryside's all going away. All going away." She shifts in her chair, because her back hurts. "The whole world, it's going downhill. Seems like it to me."

And then, I know this is selfish but I can't help it – I find myself thinking, will my end be like this? Sad, bored, scared, and stuck full of catheters? Because that's how it is for so many people. Even when you have your children and grandchildren and great-grandchildren to visit, you're still in a hospital where people go to die, where nobody has ever looked around and said, my, what a beautiful place you have here. And maybe there won't be visitors. Maybe I'll have outlived Jennifer, and maybe my children will be old themselves, or busy with their lives and with raising kids, the vital business of the living. And there I will be, clutching some get-well cards and staring at the fluorescent lighting.

Oh, I know, the British with their cheap new buildings and worn old ones, and their sad little economies, might seem more morose than most in their final dying places, but is it even so different back home? If I am alone and bedridden someday in a California hospital, will I be able to see the sky from my bed? The sun? The grass? To see other people, living normal lives outside, people who aren't having blood samples drained from them every four hours?

Ivor and my aunt Frances have been taking care of Nan and are closer to her than anyone else in the family; there is really not much to be done by anyone else, and nothing to be done for much longer in any case. But Morgan's little body is cooled and active again, and Jennifer and I want to make a visit to Nan before we leave Reading and go home.

It's not visiting hours, the head nurse lectures us when we arrive, for Nan is still getting her bath. We wait on a little lawn outside, which is accessed by a French door from the Nuffield wing; this is where dying people go to look at the sky, the grass, to feel the wind and bugs on their skin, to feel the manifestations of ordinariness that they will soon lose. The sun warms Jennifer's long blond hair, which I am absentmindedly brushing with my fingers as we watch our son, who is goose-stepping on some flagstones. Wherever there are hard surfaces – manhole covers are an especially big hit in the Morgan Parade – he will immediately abandon any grass and proceed to tap-dance on the most injurious surface available.

"Mrs. Thick can see you now."

She is delighted to see Morgan, of course: "The prize of the family," she says over and over. Morgan looks at her a little, hides his face in my armpit, and then takes an enormous interest in the custard cream biscuits on her table. She lets him have all he wants, and I make a mental note to ask Ivor to bring more for her.

"He looks just like his father," she says. Morgan eyes her from behind his cookie. He does look just like me. And I look just like my mother, Nan's daughter. Something is being saved here: a certain shape of the earlobe, a peculiarly elfin expression during sleep. These come from my grandmother's side of the family. Her grandmother left them to her when she died, as did her grandmother, going back generations into Gaul and Wales and back up to whatever god-forsaken steppe or glacier my ancestors crawled away from. We have saved these tokens of humanity. Are they worth saving? Do they mean anything? Maybe not. They just are. But I wonder – perhaps the sight of family, the family look, is some consolation to my grandmother. Like every generation before her, she has passed some faint trace of herself along.

"It's noon," Jennifer says softly.

Ivor will be outside for us now, waiting to take us to the train station. We say our farewells and then walk up the long hallway out of ward, which my Nan's bed is at one end of; she can see us walking away.

"Good-bye. Good-bye," she says.

Jennifer is carrying Morgan, and he is looking back over her shoulder, staring silently and without expression at this old woman whom he will never know. His head bobs up and down slightly with each maternal step, nodding a little with each footfall, saying over and over:

Bye bye. Bye bye. Bye bye.

Chapter Eight
Is Thinking About It

WHEN WE GET back to Hay and trudge up the long stairs to The Apartment, Diana leans out the back door of her store.

"I believe you have a new fan," she says, handing a letter to me. Once we get up to our living room, I tear the envelope open:

Paul Collins
C/o Pemberton's Bookshop
Hay-on-Wye
Hfds.

Dear Paul,

I am prepared to pay you to organise eight bays in the Net House.

Care should be taken in thinking of the physical, as well as electronic reality. Both are calculated to stimulate the return visit and a permanent valuable e-mail mailing list in as many specialities as possible.

Liz Meres will be available to help you and my staff may be able to offer assistance with your housing problem. Sid Wilding has helped in the past.

Yours sincerely,
Richard Booth

Jennifer is looking over my shoulder.

"Yes," I sigh. "Our housing problem."

The next day we are to go to Broad Street, to a place so old that it is simply known in town as First House. But we are not meeting the agent. We are meeting the owner. The agent isn't even going to be there, which makes them not much of an agent, if you ask me. Why else have an agent except to avoid awkward pauses and guilty feelings when you knock down the owner's asking price, or when you decide that the house isn't right for you? What else is an agent but a buffer, a thick metal guardplate, between your tender digits and the grinding gears of market forces?

And so I stare at the door of Judy Heath. I am alone, for Jen and Morgan are still en route. I knock downward on the door, which is just below street level, and then after awkward greetings I duck and walk inside.

It's perfect.

Or anyway, it's not perfect, but it is well maintained.

Mrs. Heath is in her late fifties, I guess. And the house?

"I'd say it's about, oh, four hundred years old," she says. "Late sixteenth century."

There are exposed beams, and odd rounded bits where the walls join, windows between rooms, creaky wooden boarding. It is an *experienced* house. And yet they've kept it in nice shape, except for the decor, which is about what you'd expect of an older English couple.

"I like that old piano," I say.

"Family heirloom, I'm afraid," she apologizes. "My husband thinks I'm barmy, but it will go with us. I couldn't part with it."

"Of course, I understand."

And I do. Pianos constitute a curious and discrete part of a family's furniture; for they are nearly immovable, and so dominating of a space that they define the room that they are in. I love pianos – all pianos are good, even the bad ones – and we were miserable when we had to leave a San Francisco friend holding Jen's most treasured family possession, a beautiful century-old Mason and Hamlin upright. But staring at this wall, I can see a new home for it.

"Hello?"

I look back and see Jen bending down with Morgan to look in through the front doorway.

Now we tour the building in earnest. It is a tight little stone house, cheap to heat, and rock-sturdy. The bedrooms are at least twelve feet square – huge for a house this old. It is a curiosity of British homes that, even when built on a sprawling estate, they will have impossibly small rooms. And when they are not built on sprawling estates, rooms are *smaller* than impossible. This is a land of dismal six-by-eight bedrooms and cheerless ten-by-twelve living rooms, even when there is no need for such stinginess; perhaps it is a sort of national hair shirt worn for the overexpansiveness of empires past.

Though there are truly impossibly small rooms in this world, worse than any I can imagine, worse than when I was holed up in a three-by-seven converted closet in San Francisco. A haunting passage in James St. John's 1831 book, *Journal of a Residence in Normandy*, describes the plight of a Dutch newspaper editor named Dubourg. Dubourg ran an article that eventually made its way to the French court and greatly offended Louis XIV, who stationed a secret agent in Holland to worm into the editor's confidence. Dubourg's new-found "friend," after two years undercover, convinced the hapless Dutchman to go on a merry jaunt across the border into France – whereupon a company of the king's soldiers, kept in perpetual readiness for the trap, instantly seized the fellow. Dubourg was locked for twenty years in a rat-infested wooden cage, never again seeing another human face save that of his jailer. He did, however, create some heartbreaking art:

> Some faint rays of light, just such as enable cats and owls to mouse, found their way into the dungeon; and by their aid, Dubourg, whom accident or humanity had put in possession of an old nail, and who inherited the passion of his countrymen for flowers, contrived to sculpture roses and other flowers upon the beams of his cage.

But Europe is more civilized today, I suppose. Come to England and visit Warwick Castle, and you will see the following sign posted:

> **Torture Chamber Not Suitable**
> **for Wheelchair Users**

There is almost no backyard at First House – just a patio, a few planters, and a crooked little shed.

"That shed" – Judy points us inside – "is the old privy, from before they had plumbing here."

The floor is concrete now, but I look down anyway. What I expect to see, I can't even tell you. When you inform someone that *this used to be a toilet,* they will always look down. It doesn't matter if you're talking about yesterday's campsite or an ancient Roman pit toilet; somehow we still expect something.

Jennifer and I thank Mrs. Heath, and we walk up Broad Street with Morgan in tow.

"I'm sold."

"Me too."

"Good. Let's buy it."

Only, we can't quite afford the price they are asking. This is a problem. But three doors up from First House is the man to solve all problems: Martin Beales, Solicitor.

Home buyers in Britain don't have their own agents, but they do have solicitors to help handle the paperwork; and so we trudge upstairs on creaky steps to Mr. Beales. There have always been two solicitors in town; the other's office is across the street, poised as if ready to come to blows with this one. And so they have: I had heard once that some infamous local crime between the rivals happened in these offices perhaps a century ago, and I try to imagine the sound the boots of the local constables made thudding up this very stairwell.

"Please, come on in."

Martin Beales looks as if we have just woken him up bleary-eyed from a slumber of several days in duration. His room is dark, overflowing with documents, nary a computer in sight; yellowing light peeps in from a window and upon rough-hewn flooring. It would all be listed in a movie script as *Solicitor in ancient Welsh village*.

"We're thinking of buying First House," Jennifer says as we sit down, "and – "

"First House? I didn't know it was for sale."

"It is – for 144,500 pounds."

"I . . ." He stops, leans back in his chair, and muses. "I couldn't tell you what a fair price would be for houses in Hay. But I'll tell you what. I remember when these buildings in this town were selling for twelve thousand pounds. Think about it. Think about it."

I mention a second house, and he frowns slightly: what about the business next to it? What if its elderly owner dies and it gets redeveloped into something nasty? What if the business becomes popular and is overrun with tourists? What if this owner becomes senile and the property is overrun with rats?

"Think about it," he says. "Think about it."

And then he stops to think about it.

Okay, then. We propose a third house that we've heard is for sale. Ah, but that one might be dangerous for children. And what of the pub nearby?

"And I don't know how it doesn't get robbed blind," he sighs, and adds sharply, *"Only drink the bottled beer there."*

"Why's tha – "

"Think about it. Think about it."

Very little ever happens in Hay-on-Wye. And I think I know why: because whenever a resident had a plan to do something, they asked Martin first. And ever since then they have been thinking about it, thinking about it.

"But" – he shrugs rhetorically – "what do I know about homes here?"

A great deal, I suspect.

"I'm just acting on your behalf," he continues. "You must decide first. The market says if you pay 144.5 for a house, then it is worth 144.5 . . . to you. But what if you want to sell in a year? Think about it. Think about it."

Morgan is straining to reach out of his stroller: *eh, ehhh, bbbbooo* . . . ah, I see. There are toy trucks in this window.

H. R. Grant & Son is a wonderful store dating back to the 1840s, perhaps the oldest business on Castle Street, and I stop by every day to pick up the London papers. There is a little of everything inside – magazines ranging from *The Economist* to *Hello!,* candy bars, and local books. But most important of all are the toys in the window. I lift up and cram the stroller through the narrow half-door, crunch past a display of Wye River postcards – "Afternoon. You all right there?" says the shopmistress, and I grunt, yes, yes, I'm okay – and then I grab the dump truck for Morgan. He will spin its wheels and then wham it against the side of his stroller for at least five minutes, which buys me some time to look around the store.

The newsracks are nearly toppling over with home decorating and DIY magazines. But décor magazines are different here. In the States, glossy home magazines reveal how fabulous your living room might look without the inconvenience of actual occupants; unless you are in the habit of keeping a light meter on your nightstand and setting up umbrella reflectors on either side of your headboard, you will never wake up in a house that looks as if it came out of an American magazine. But houses in British décor magazines actually look like a house you've been in; they are your house this morning, in fact, as you left it on your way to work. Look, in that picture: there is where you dropped your cell phone!

It all makes their domestic dreams a little – well, *homely* seems like the right word, but also recognizable, attainable. The living rooms in their magazines have *televisions*. British magazines give advice for homes with thatched roofs – water reed is the best kind of thatching, in case you are wondering – and where to site your rabbit hutch. They hold contest giveaways of tea cozies and wicker baskets. They tell you how to dye your own fabrics. American décor magazines are for those who hire someone else to do the decorating: British ones are for those who do it themselves. And they photograph all these rooms with natural light, which, it being Britain, means no light at all.

Next to these magazines are shelves of books. There are a number of hiking guides to the area, as we are near ramblers' trails and the Black Mountains, and there are several histories of Hay itself – an impressive showing for a town so small, but not surprising in a place where citizens sit out the winter months with little else to do but stare at the towering heaps of books around them.

I notice another book on the shelf, one I'd never even glanced at before.

Beales?

I pull down the book, and there he is: Martin Beales. Even the people who don't sell books around here have to at least *write* them, it seems. Our solicitor's book is a handsome paperback titled *The Hay Poisoner;* and for a moment I wonder about his advice to drink only bottled beer at the pub.

I settle back into the living room at The Apartment, and with one eye on Morgan as he spins his toy truck around in circles, I leaf through *The Hay Poisoner*. It's the sort of tale that Agatha Christie might have written, except . . . it is not a tale. It is the true history of the crime of which I had been dimly aware of that occurred in Beales's office. In the 1920s there were two solicitor's offices in Hay: that of Major Herbert Armstrong, a war veteran who occupied the offices used today by Beales, and that of Robert Griffiths and Oswald Martin, now occupied by Gabb & Co., directly across the street. Armstrong had both friends and enemies in town, depending on whose side of a case he had worked on; he certainly was not liked by Fred Davies, the town chemist.

Major Armstrong's wife, though apparently much loved by the major, became unmanageably sickly and mentally unstrung by 1920 and died the following year; not long afterward, the major invited his rival solicitor to tea. Would Mr. Martin have one of the buttered scones? Major Armstrong insisted on it.

"Excuse fingers," he famously said, passing one to Martin.

Martin became violently ill later that day; his wife soon became sickened from a box of chocolate sent anonymously through the post to their home, which, incredibly, they had *eaten*. (What trusting souls people were back then!) Two of the remaining chocolates appeared to have been surreptitiously drilled into. The town doctor, suspicious, had Martin's urine and the chocolates analyzed. The lab results came back: arsenic. Police seized Armstrong from his law offices and threw him into jail, and the body of Mrs. Armstrong was disinterred. She too proved to have arsenic in her body; and so Major Herbert Armstrong went to the scaffold on May 31, 1922.

Armstrong – whose rather shaky conviction is still a matter of debate – does get the occasional new companion in the local gallery of rogues. A few years back, a group of enterprising fellows in the area were found to be running a *counterfeiting ring*.* Like any good creators of capital, these counterfeiters avoided too much vertical integration by diversifying their business interests, for the police found that they were also running a *pornography ring*. It must have made for difficult filming; imagine how long it took the local actors to pull off their wellies and their tight tweed jackets.

More than other villages of its size, Hay seems prone to such rollicking good crimes. One of the properties currently for sale is the town dentist's office. There was, a few years back, a hostage situation in this dentist's office with a fellow wielding a weapon. Given the array of drills and needles the dentist was armed with, surely it was an uneven standoff. But perhaps such mishaps are in the nature of both this town and this country. A popular bookstore in town is called Murder and Mayhem, and even the town historian, Kate Clarke, holds a day job as a crime writer. For it is the British, after all, who invented crime writing as we know it. This is a country where Thomas De Quincey could write a classic of sangfroid with an essay titled "On Murder Considered as One of the Fine Arts." And he starts his section on murdered philosophers with the most perfect opening line in belles lettres:

"Hobbes – but why, or on what principle, I could never under-stand – was not murdered."

---

* Counterfeiters operate only in rings, never in straight lines or polygons.

Chapter Nine
Discovers the Wit and Wisdom
of Elmore Hubbard

BOOTH'S GENERAL manager is waiting in the stacks for me, looking over it all with a sort of morbid humor.

He shakes my hand. "You must be Paul."

"Yes!"

"You'll meet your colleagues in due time. Richard collects odd-balls, you see. I'm the only normal one here." He smiles conspiratorially.

I cannot tell from his expression whether he is joking, but he is already steering me to the shelves that I have been assigned.

"About my creating a new American lit section . . ."

"Oh." He waves his hand dismissively. "Richard gets enthused over things, then changes his mind – but his goal is always the same. He is an anarchist." The manager nods at the bookshelf signs around me. "See those signs? That's your predecessor. He made them before leaving. Leaving in *disgust,* I should think. You see, I am the manager of a thing that is unmanageable." He gives a helpless shrug of the shoulders.

"And if I have any questions . . . ?"

"You'll have to ask the fellow on the first floor. You can't miss him; he's the one-eyed man in a red cape."

Then he leaves me alone to ponder my task.

This is a building filled with books. In stacks, in boxes, on shelves, on slippery collapsed snowdrifts of paper and bindings that spill out into the aisles, labeled and unlabeled, priced and unpriced, books books books. The first thing, I decide, is to weed out everything that does not belong in this section, which has been marked U.S. FICTION AND ESSAYS. There are many books here that are not fiction, are not essays, are not even from the United States.

The 1958 minutes of the Canadian Parliament? No.

The Happy Hooker? No.

A 1974 *AAA Road Guide* to Texas? No.

The Incubator Baby? Why, yes, actually. It is a 1906 Ellis Butler novel.

The shelves are packed, and I am riddling them with holes, letting the remaining books breathe again. At first I handle the books carefully, as I always do with old books. But a couple hours and a few hundred books later, I'm just tossing books, and they hit the floor with a satisfying thud. Soon the whole floor is covered, two and three volumes deep, and I'm walking and slipping on them underfoot, like a scree. It makes no difference: the floor of the entire building is already strewn with books. Stacks of Artemus Ward, Sam Slick, *London Illustrated News* magazines from 1920 in mint condition, *Scribner's* magazines from the 1870s, spellers from 1842 – it's all here.

Today I find two great books in this annex, for just £2 each: a perfectly preserved, dust-jacketed slab of 1929 Social Realism about an immigrant baker, titled *Hunky* ("In America everything goes fast. It is because the country has got yeast in it"), and a *Dickens Dictionary of London*. The latter is an 1884 guide for dwellers in that city, with everything from the hours of local shops to advice for householders on how to avoid getting robbed by a stellar array of London con men: by sham delivery services, conniving scissors sharpeners, cutlery-stealing glaziers, and above all else by the gas company. Even cast-iron possessions are not safe unless bolted down: "If the pattern of your mudscraper pleases you, or you attach any importance to its possession, it is well not to leave it unsecured out of doors after dusk."

Sometimes I find, in completely wrong or unnamed sections, little clusters of prime choices, often covered in dust. These are volumes squirreled away and then forgotten by other book nuts, perhaps years ago; they are in Manhattan or Melbourne or Milan, kicking themselves for not buying that one copy of *The Masque of Poets*. I merrily raid their stashes, of course, and it works both ways; on a previous trip, when I was nearly out of money in another bookshop, I secreted a first edition of *A Key to Uncle Tom's Cabin* behind a wormy set of educational regulations. And when we visited six months later with cash in hand, it was *gone*. What were the odds?

I often wish I had that book; it is unique. After getting tired of slaveowners attacking *Uncle Tom's Cabin,* Harriet Beecher Stowe hurled *A Key* back at them: a justification of why *Uncle Tom's Cabin* was written, an explication of each character in the book, and an assemblage of news clippings to show that the depravities of slavery were no mere fiction. I cannot name another novelist before Stowe who peeled back the skin of a novel to show us its beating and breathing organs. We are used to this today, in our *Making of* world of self-reference that we can never really turn back from, and theologians were used to it before Stowe, with their endless hermeneutics upon the meaning and making of every word of Scripture. But no one had thought to apply this scalpel to art. Nobody took much notice of Stowe's innovation at the time, but perhaps no one has done it better ever since; for her literary scholarship was written *to save lives*. Who can top that?

My shift is nearing an end, and suddenly I notice a low rafter over my head at the end of the aisle. Looking up – why, I can just barely see that someone has secretly wedged a slim volume atop it, where no one will ever see.

Mine mine mine.

I hop up and snatch at it – and down rains a shower of dirt and mouse droppings into my face.

I sputter and spit, slapping the germs away from my lips.

"Ugh! ugh! ugh!" I yell. "Hantavirus! Shit shit *shit!*" – which indeed it is. Then I look at my filthy little tome: *The Wit and Wisdom of Elmore Hubbard.*

I stuff it back into the rafter crack.

I do not meet a single other employee or customer in the building for the rest of the day. Perhaps they're all at the pub, for directly across the street and scarcely thirty feet from my shelves stands the Wheatsheaf. The first time Jennifer looked inside this pub, a bookseller was belting out "Don't Be Cruel" and "American Pie," with a tableful of colleagues watching in a mixture of pride and horror. For the fellow had filled the jukebox with change – *there will be no intermissions in tonight's performance.*

But now the Wheatsheaf is renovating. The pool table and fruit machine area are sealed off, being absorbed into a restaurant or some sort of more pleasant venue. This will be an improvement. For – no travel writer will ever tell you this – many British pubs really are not much fun at all. You will read of pubs filled with curious local characters, folk musicians, and entire families out to dine on hearty fare, and such places do exist – student pubs are fun, as are ancient pubs with hidden snugs and Guinness Steak Pie. But go out to the suburbs or the countryside and seek out a signboard that reads KING'S HEAD or THE BLACK HORSE or THE PIG AND ROSE, and you will sit in a twilight scene lit only by the flashing bulbs of the sad little fruit machines, munching on a greasy packet of prawn crisps and thinking to yourself that the signboard outside should instead read:

> ## QUIET DESPERATION
> *Served 10 A.M. – 11 P.M. daily*

The Wheatsheaf was where locals went to do their hard drinking, and it gave the place this slightly weary edge. But now it's all plaster dust and timbers and plastic sheeting, and so after work we make a family outing to Kilvert's, which has in any case become our favorite pub simply because it has a big garden for Morgan to run around in.

When we get to Kilvert's, an argument is going on outside the entrance between a couple about the same age as us, an entirely ordinary-looking man, and a spike-haired woman.

"Oh, come back," the man says.

"I *hate* Hay," she spits. "It's a dump. There's nothing here. There's no life for me here."

She is wearing a T-shirt that reads, in full:

PISS OFF WANKER

"That's not true," he says.

"Yes, it is." She stalks out into the Bull Ring and yells back at him, "It's *boring* here."

He runs after her, and they disappear around a corner.

Drinking resumes inside the pub – show's over – and Jennifer and I look at each other.

"Jeez," she says. "Why wouldn't she fit in here?"

"I don't know. Not enough books about pissing and wanking?"

And yet here is the strange thing: they're almost the only other people of our age that I've seen in this town. We came from a San Francisco neighborhood full of new parents fresh out of grad school and art school; but somehow, out here, we are . . . alone.

Mick, a book dealer with two shops in town, hails us as we reach the garden. We stagger across, balancing our child, a bag of toys, wipes, and sippy cups.

"How's the search?"

"Well," I tell him, "our househunting has hit a snag."

"Oh?"

"The appraisal for First House came back at ninty-eight, but the Heaths want one forty-four."

"One forty-four for First House?" he says incredulously. "They're dreaming."

Morgan toddles to the other side of the garden and I jog after him. There is a cat here, black and white, parading about with tail arched up and flicking. Morgan wants to grab the cat and hug it like a squeeze bottle of meows; I hold him back.

"Stroke, Morgan. Stroke the kitty. Gentle."

He barely touches the tip of the tail. He is smiling, all eight teeth showing, and looks up at me, delighted.

Raaow, the cat says.

And then it starts: the giggle. Morgan is giggling at this creature, the likes of which he has seen only in pictures before – the very *idea* of a cat is funny to him – and then he is giggling uncontrollably. And then I start laughing too – it *is* hilarious, somehow – but also I am listening. Breaking through his baby giggle, which is high-pitched and sweet, is an occasional huskier laugh. Perhaps because he has never laughed so hard before, but I can hear a child. Not a baby, but a little boy. Only just.

And then it is gone. The cat slinks away under some bushes, spooked by the maniacally laughing baby, and Morgan toddles back toward the tables, wavering a little with each step, tugging on his overall straps, and looking back at me with a smile.

Jen is calling First House's agent, and I am in the next room taking a bath. This is because there is no point in taking showers in Britain. In the United States, water pressure *presses;* in Britain, water pressure *sucks.* Every shower in Britain has some sort of Heath Robinson mechanism – he is their equivalent of Rube Goldberg, only Robinson had to work with metric wrenches and 220 current – and he devised for all British showers a cheap plastic box with tubes that go nowhere and buttons that do nothing, except for the one that will scald you.* Apparently it is some kind of filtration system for removing any pleasure one might have in washing. When I was a little boy in America, the pounding water pressure would allow me to stand with my eyes closed in the shower and imagine that I was flying a wounded P-57 back to base, with rain whipping into the cockpit; or to pretend that I was getting heroically smashed against a brick wall by a water cannon wielded by riot police. But I'm not sure what British boys can imagine in their showers. Perhaps they pretend that they are standing under a rusted and leaking pipe in an unlit boiler room. Or that someone is weeing on them from a great height.

So instead I'm in a deep, enameled, thick-lipped Victorian claw-footer, the kind that you can plunge down into and let the water close over your head, and the tub conducts all the internal sounds of the house – after the churning of bathwater subsides – the efficient hum of the water heater, the squirting rush of water pipes and drains, the groaning of ancient steps in another part of the building. You can hear

---

* American patent law requires that inventions demonstrate *utility;* British patent law does not. This fact may be the Rosetta stone to understanding British household appliances.

everything in an old house through the bathtub. Everything, that is, but the people in it. Voices don't carry, for some reason.

Woosh.

"But the valuation was ninety-eight thousand."

" "

"I know, but aren't you legally obliged to convey our offer to them?"

" "

"Yes, but – "

Woosh.

If I listen closely, slow the beating of my heart, I can hear the hum of fluorescent lights in the bookshop below. Hmm. One of the bulbs needs replacing, I'd say.

Woosh.

"We like the house very much, yes."

" "

"No. We are *disinclined* to offer more."

The phone hangs up, and Jennifer comes in. She has been doing all the work; I, meanwhile, haven't even rinsed and repeated yet. Not that it matters; unlike a shower, a bath does not so much clean you as simply redistribute your dirt more evenly.

"So?"

"Did you hear that?"

"Some of it."

"He said *you can't put a price on that house because it's unique.*"

"That's an interesting theory for a realtor to espouse."

"Then he said the surveyors were wrong – both of them. And the comparison house was wrong. And that the market's on the way up, never mind what the papers say."

"Did he say anything else?"

"Yes. He said he'll call back."

But he never does.

Chapter Ten
Wishes Life Would Leave It Alone

I'VE BEEN TO Spar, the health food store, the bakery, and now the Londis.

"Where's the bread?" I blurt out.

"Pardon?"

"The bread," I repeat, pointing to the empty racks in their storefront window. "I've been in every shop in town and I can't seem to find any."

"*Oh,*" the Londis clerks say in unison.

Yes?

"The petrol strike," one of them says.

"What about it?"

"It's stopped deliveries. Hasn't been any bread delivered today or yesterday."

"So" – this takes a moment to sink in – "you have no bread?"

"I'm afraid not."

And I just stand there a moment, like a clubbed seal.

"Do you know where I could find some?"

"Ahh . . . ," the clerks harmonize, and ponder this.

"No," one finally says.

I poke around their store shelves, not quite knowing what to do. The fresh milk is gone too. It just seems so strange to be denied this;

to an American, finding empty shelves in a market, to be told that *you can't buy something,* is a little like waking up and being told that gravity has been switched off until further notice. It is no accident that the local supermarket in old *Freak Brothers* comics was called Food Flood: in America, not only are stores never out of goods, they are absolutely awash in them. Freestanding pyramidal displays of tinned goods just waiting to get knocked over – that staple of low-quality movies and sitcoms – are our culture's visual shorthand for this. Even though no actual supermarket displays their goods in this way, it is understood that the pyramid symbolizes the notion that you can actually slip, fall down, and get *buried in product* at an American store.

I'm sure the pharaohs would understand.

So now there's no chance of my finding a ring loaf. This is a wonderfully light kind of round, corrugated bread that I have become addicted to. But I find, to my joy, that the Londis has frozen bread dough, an item that the less savvy hunter-gatherers have overlooked. I stock up and flee back to The Apartment with my frigid haul and watch the TV news while a loaf defrosts and then bakes.

The strike is all over the news today. Truckers have created rolling barricades and have blocked off the entrances of petroleum refineries; and rather than send out a National Guard to gas and club them, the British government does . . . well, nothing really. The truckers are protesting gas prices, because Britain has some of the highest in the world, despite sitting atop a North Sea oil field. This is due to the enormous tax the government imposes on every liter.

The prime minister appears on the BBC and insists that his hands are tied on this matter. He does not attack the strikers and call them morons or bullies; he merely reiterates that the petrol tax is vital. But he makes no explanation of why the petrol tax is so vital here. It's not for the revenue it provides, although that's certainly why politicians love it so. It's because it keeps the British off the roads. A higher percentage of British households than U.S. households either do not own a car or have only one car. This is partly due to their lower standard of living, but it is also a negatively reinforced social responsibility – who wants three cars, or even one SUV, when fueling them costs a fortune? Public transport, in turn, is much more heavily invested in here than in the United States, with all the social and environmental benefits that follow.

Americans are horrified when they see British fuel taxes; our citizens whine like a cloud of gnats whenever our prices approach a couple of dollars a gallon – which is, by the way, still much cheaper than bottled water. But the British petrol tax is one of the most responsible laws that any Western country has ever passed, an unsung act of political heroism that no American politician would ever dare to attempt. (Though the United Kingdom is no match for Denmark, which imposes both VAT and a *103 percent* registration tax on new cars.) Even UK public transport puts the United States to shame. There is scarcely a town in Britain that you can't reach somehow, eventually, via public transit.

Back in America, I sometimes wondered whether my wife and I were the only people in the country without cars, without licenses even; she's never had one, and I neglected to renew mine years ago. When people would tell us that something was nearby, Jennifer and I would look at each other and silently think, yes, it's nearby, *for car people*. Not owning a car shapes your conception of the United States in weird ways, analogous to Saul Steinberg's famous map of New York and the rest of the country. For Not-Car-Having People, the United States consists of New York, Boston, San Francisco, Seattle, and Chicago, and a series of transcontinental stops following the Amtrak and Greyhound routes between the aforementioned destinations; one mile to either side of these routes, the ground drops away beneath your feet into chasms of inaccessibility. Should you make it to a smaller city, your experience of that city is limited to the downtown and adjacent areas; everything outside is Hinterland.

The entire states of Arizona and Florida do not even exist.

"Have you seen Richard Booth's book?" Diana asks me when I walk into the store to pay the week's rent.

"No, I haven't. I only just started Martin Beales's."

"Yes. Well, Richard has one out too, I believe. An autobiography."

She way she pronounces *Richard* leads me to believe that she will not be reading it herself.

"I'll have to look it up," I say. "Oh, here's the rent."

We have not set up a checking account yet, and so I always hand over a wad of cash from the ATM, which makes it all feel strangely illegal, as if I'm paying for a shipment of bathtub gin. Though I suppose only an American would bother to connect alcohol with crime; the British looked upon our Prohibition back then, and on our alcohol laws today, with the same sort of puzzled bemusement they often have at American mores. Americans are never entirely satisfied with having alcohol around, or entirely happy when it is gone. "The Los Angeles Police," the *Guardian* dryly noted in 1920, "baffled by the successful [getaway] disappearance of their Californian malefactors, put it all down to Prohibition. Without the handicap of alcohol, they announce in all solemnity, the wits of the criminal move far too briskly for a mere policeman to apprehend his person. 'Burglars now work with their brains unaffected by drink,' they explain with regret."

After paying my rent, I head up to Hay Castle with Morgan; it is a fine day out as he rides on my shoulders, batting my head with a carrot stick. The streets are sunny but not too hot, and a little quieter than usual for noontime. It takes a moment for me to remember why this is: almost nobody is driving their car during the petrol strike.

In a field at the bottom of the castle hill is a motley collection of rusted metal bookshelves and clapped-out old hardcover books, all left to sit in the open air. This is the end of the line for the printed word, the place where absolutely unsalable books from Booth's stock wind up. HONESTY BOOKSHOP, a sign announces over a slotted lockbox, BOOKS 50 PENCE. These unfortunate volumes are not brought inside at the end of the day; they just sit out in the wind and the rain until some buyer takes pity on them and drops a few pence into the unmanned box, or until the action of sun and moisture upon the paper decomposes the books into pulp.

Morgan runs around the field, stopping to inspect the decaying books, then zippering back and forth across the path again. We're there twenty minutes and have the whole place to ourselves, which is great.

"Ahh . . . ahhh . . ."

He wants to climb the steps up to the castle itself, and I want to talk him out of it.

"Look, Morgan." I gesture wildly back at the shelves. "Books! Books!" – as if that means anything in Hay.

"Okay," I finally say, steering him away from the rickety stairs. "Let's go the other way."

Morgan and I walk up the rocky back driveway to the castle. I'd been to the castle at least a dozen times before I noticed that it had another field – the size of a football field, which is the only unit of land measurement that an American has – hidden away behind it.

There is a wall and a gate between the driveway and the field, and a sign reading PRIVATE. Not until much later did I discern, upon looking more closely at the sign, that it also said in faded marker, *Tickets for entry 50p in Castle bookshop*. When I went in – it was cold and raining that day – and requested a ticket to go into their backyard, I was met by a blank stare; evidently it had been a long time since anybody had asked to go out there.

Morgan and I go behind the castle every day now. This is where Morgan and I play, alone, away from the world, in the brooding shadows of a ruin. The castle is fantastically grim from the back: toppled battlements and crumbling stone walls, leaded windows twisted into filigree by the heat of the fire that gutted the place; and over it all, thick layers of ivy. There is a rubbish heap of stones and fallen mortar in one spot, and in the middle of it a smashed wooden buggy. It is the coolest place in the world for a piggyback ride.

We run across the lawn, the castle looming behind us and the Black Mountains and Hay Bluff bouncing in our line of sight with each step. Morgan pumps his elbows up and down and makes his little monkey noises.

In the middle of this back field, of course, are even more piles of thousands of books: great big dead bodies of books, covered with a dirty blue tarp that is weighted down with cracked-off bits of masonry. The wind has whipped up one corner of a tarp and is flinging it back and forth; underneath I can see an old 1950s binding of an Agatha Christie book peeping out.

Every bookstore in this town is toppling under the weight of cardboard boxes of books, all marked mysteriously TAPON – FRANCE.

Morgan has finally worn out both of us, and I carry him on my shoulders back up the dirt path to the gate and load him into the carriage, and we totter away down the old cobblestone drive. A breeze descends on the looming ruins of the castle behind us and whistles through its ancient empty windows. A few clouds pass over the sun, and we walk home.

There is some basic human need to read through other people's journals; otherwise, why would they leave them in unlocked desks? Sitting brazenly in the bottom of a drawer, barely hidden beneath a ream of paper, a stapler, and a Trapper Keeper? That, at least, was my reasoning as a teenager. But now, as an adult, it is unseemly to go rooting about in people's desks, under their mattresses, and on their upper closet shelves – I must settle for published journals. I'm sorting through the rest of the fiction and essay section today at Booth's, and a number of the misfiled books are journals by British writers. One in particular catches my eye: *The Journal of a Disappointed Man,* by W. P. Barbellion. How can you not open a book with that title? For I once came across a book in a library titled *Recollections of a Happy Life;* it was about a century old, and it had never been checked out. You may wish to infer something from this.

Our disappointed man was a remarkable self-taught naturalist who worked for the British Museum during World War I. His fascination with nature is evident from the very first entry in his journal, at age thirteen:

> *January 3, 1903.* Am writing an essay on the life-history of insects and have abandoned the idea of writing on "How Cats Spend Their Time."

His journal progresses with all the violent loves and hatreds and despairs of young adulthood ("I should like to blow up his face with dynamite," he says of one acquaintance); meanwhile, he is constantly dogged with illness. "Zoology is all I want," he complains in a 1910 entry. "Why won't Life leave me alone?" His doctors largely dismissed his symptoms as a nervous disposition. They were not: Barbellion died of multiple sclerosis in 1919, at the age of thirty. Most of his writings were published posthumously, to be lauded at last by the likes of H. G. Wells.

But there is another journal that I discover today, too . . . an unpublished one, this time. It is a curiosity of Booth's that the vast sweeping motions employed by indiscriminate librarians and estate auctioneers will cause all sorts of extraneous items to be thrown into the shipping boxes: people's address books, bits of library shelving, committee minutes from local Kiwanis meetings, and so forth.

In a box marked MASSACHUSETTS I find a handwritten journal kept by someone named Robert Spade and dated 1987. His journal is a cheap, marbled black-and-white composition book written in ballpoint pen, what you might normally see in an American ninth-grader's schoolbag, and yet here it is in the Welsh countryside, crammed between two moldy volumes of the Massachusetts census records.

At one point our journalist spends an entire page detailing that morning's squeezing of a pimple. ("It wasn't really ready to burst," he sagely concludes.) Later, writing about an unnamed woman, he describes her thus: "She looks great for her age. She's a looker. She is a rolling donut." I close the notebook and set it back between the leatherbound volumes. Perhaps I will find the address of this Mr. Spade someday and send him his old journal from out of the blue, with nothing but an enigmatic Welsh postmark – "The *hell?*" he will say – to indicate whence it emanated.

Who knows where juvenilia goes? I have moved into houses or apartments where there were old homework assignments and crayon scribblings to be found among the broken tennis rackets and lawn chairs and other junk abandoned by previous tenants. I don't know where my own homework papers and scribblings are, either; probably at the bottom of a landfill.

And no copy exists, so far as I am aware, of *Doors of Sleep,* the first book that I ever wrote. I wrote it when I was fifteen, in a desperate attempt to imitate Kurt Vonnegut. I composed it late each night at my boarding school, after my roommates went to sleep; later, when I found them and other students quoting its passages aloud and hooting in hilarity over my ineptitude, I realized they'd been going through my desk. It was humiliating, especially considering how politely discreet I'd been in going through *their* desks. I drilled a hole through my notebook and took to chaining it to the underside of my iron bed frame.

Later that spring, a Very Famous Playwright visited my school for several days; it was that kind of school, I guess, though I was quite ungrateful for it. Before he'd arrived, they'd herded us into Memorial Hall to watch the old black-and-white film with Big Stars that had been made from his Big Play, and so we all sat on the wooden benches in the dark making farting sounds and punching each other. Anyway, then the Very Famous Playwright spent three afternoons fielding the same question over and over from well-scrubbed boys in blazers and ties – "How can you be a *Democrat?*" we'd pester – and he would erupt into a deep sigh whenever anyone said that they wanted to be a writer.

"People who want to be writers don't become writers," he explained. "You write because you *have* to."

We all scratched our heads at that one.

Our English teacher told us that if we gave Mr. V. F. Playwright our writing, he would read it and comment upon it. So, blissfully unaware that perhaps my piece was a little longer than what they'd expected, I turned in the handwritten manuscript of my first novel, complete with the hole drilled in for my bike chain.

None of the students ever got their stuff back. Somewhere out there in 1985 – either in the teacher's desk, the VFP's attic, or more likely in a trash can at a rest stop on the Schuylkill Expressway – my first novel vanished. In retrospect, it's probably just as well. But I don't think I was quite so philosophical about it at the time.

Chapter Eleven
Judges Books by Their Covers

I LIKE WORKING at Booth's, as much as one can *like* working. Nobody takes any notice of my coming and going. I come when I am ready to work and go when I am ready to not work. I don't know if anyone even really knows that I am back here or has observed that I have begun to sort the fiction and essays into regional groups – New York, New England, Southern, Frontier, and so forth. And yet when I arrive this afternoon, I can immediately see that my sections have been tampered with. Odd little piles of books are drawn out and stacked, for no apparent reason. Even more mysteriously, next to that is a half-full can of Boddington's ale. I stare and stare at one stack until the meaning hits me. All of them have blue covers, and – *and* – all of them have authors beginning with the letter *B*. Blue . . . *B!* Well, it all makes sense now.

Doesn't it?

About every twenty minutes or so, a wizened little Irishman wanders into the book stacks. His name, he says, is Sean. He wears a tweed cap.

"So you're Richard's new fellow?"

"Yeah, hi!"

He watches me sort, then goes on carrying in boxes of books, which will go to the glacial mass that is swallowing the back of the building. These books are dumped out of the box and onto the floor. They are arriving in cargo containers from the United States, unsorted and unpriced, unknown, boxed up in whatever was handy – incongruous boxes stamped MCDONALD'S FRENCH FRIES and BOUNTY TABLE TOWELS. Some have AMERICA written on them in marker, but otherwise there's no telling what's in them.

Sean goes back out to the Booth van to get more.

"How on earth did you find petrol for the van?" I yell after him, but he can't hear me.

Eventually he shuffles back in with his boxes, like an ant building a mighty hill of sand grains. The landslide of boxes at the back of the building has already swallowed up the genealogy, military, and crime sections, which are now completely inaccessible under the crush.

Soon he is joined by a young man in dreadlocks – "Hello, I'm Stewart," he says as he slips past me – who begins pitching the empty cardboard boxes up into a sort of crow's nest, a hanging platform that is buried under chucked-up spent boxes. I watch him, and we scatter when a few boxes come crashing down.

"So" – I join him in grabbing boxes and tossing them up – "are you from around here?"

"Here? Good heavens, no. Edinburgh."

"Really? I just moved from San Francisco, myself."

"You'll find it's different here. It gets quiet in the winter. Cold, *and very quiet.*"

Then he eyes me significantly, and suddenly I feel as if I've landed the caretaker gig in *The Shining*.

Once I finish tossing boxes with Stewart, I pick through a section of rhetoric and oratory. Who reads the collected works of Daniel Webster or Henry Clay any more? And never mind Rufus Root. Anyway, amongst these I find a misfiled slim, green volume –

Princeton Verse. It is unprepossessing, a thin volume of earnestly conventional jottings from lads who had just returned from the Great War or who had just missed it. It looks like an entirely ordinary, forgettable little book from 1919.

It is not.

It is worth . . . a lot.

And the volume has not been priced. It occurs to me that if I take it up to the cashier, this bland little unpriced volume, she'll probably flip through it and say, "Oh, I don't know . . . two pounds." Or I could even just stroll out through this fire exit and innocently walk the hundred feet or so over to The Apartment.

But instead I stroll over to the main Booth building, jump up the stairs two at a time, and hand the volume to the cashier.

"Here," I say. "You might want to put this in a display case."

"Oh?"

"It's F. Scott Fitzgerald's first appearance in print. He has a poem in it. Here, see?"

She examines it, then stows it under the counter. "Yes. Right then."

I stand there a moment, waiting for something to happen. Nothing does. That's it. No klaxons sound, no balloons descend from the ceiling. I am not caller number twelve.

Nobody even cares.

Not every book at Booth's is a lost treasure. You have to sift through a lot of rubble first. The saddest sights also come today; that is, I'm looking at the poetry section. Is there anything more wrenchingly pathetic than bad poetry? Even other poets won't read it. One of the first books I pull down is an 1893 volume titled *Current Coins, Picked Up at the Railway Station,* in which S. Q. Lapius begins with the immortal invocation *"Come with me, my numismatic friend . . ."*

There is such a desperate desire in many of us to publish – to get it out there somehow, anyhow. And the greater the obstacles to publication, the more desperate the writer becomes. Just publish my poem, please. You don't even have to pay me. I pick up a slim volume, blurrily printed on cheap paper and staplebound – *The International Hall of Fame Poets;* compiled in 1969, it says, by Dr. Francis Clark Handler and the Florida State Poetry Society, Incorporated. I look inside:

> This is the SECOND of the INTERNATIONAL HALL OF FAME POETS books series. Every poet in this volume is an award winning writer of National and International stature in the poetic world.
>
> The long list of credits, awards, medals and scrolls that they have won would fill several volumes. It is suffice to say – they would NOT be in this book unless the record of their work were on file in any accredited reference book.

There is something touching in the notion that poets are accredited, and that the good ones have trophy cases full of medals and scrolls. The submissions in the volume are by Florida family doctors, Missouri retirees, anybody at all. Many poems involve pets. And they all rhyme. For a writer, there is something ineffably sad about these little productions, though they probably give the contributors some pleasure. And yet . . . is it safe to say, perhaps, that the purveyors of such anthologies, the organizers of writing contests with $30 entry fees, even the publishers of *Writer's Digest* magazine, have little actual interest in writers or writing?

Perhaps.

What is worse, I suppose, is the feeling of rubbernecking. Like most writers, I collected rejection slips for years, well over a hundred for my first short-story collection alone. And to see these twisted bodies of work buried in a shoddy binding and the quicklime of poor-quality ink – my God, they sold this shantytown as a *Hall of Fame* – all I can think of as I look at a forgotten housewife's poem is: that could have been me.

"So, this our new author," Diana pronounces as I walk into her store. "He has a book coming out in the spring. His name is *Paul Collins.*"

I look up and shake hands with a woman I've not seen in here before.

"Paul," Diana continues, "this is Clare Purcell. She organizes the Hay Festival."

"I've always wondered about the festival," I say. "There are some other writers that I'd love to talk into coming to it."

"Well! You shall have to call me, then."

One could fairly say that Clare and Diana, though not rooted in the town's past, are the faces of its future. For a town that once subsisted on butter and wool – selling it, not eating it – Hay has seen a great many changes in its economy and its populace. With the exception of the bookseller Derek Addyman, almost nobody in the town's book trade is actually from Hay. It is a town composed of refugees from London, Edinburgh, Liverpool, the States, anyplace but the Welsh countryside. The town bookbinder came from Illinois, the copy shop owner from California, and even Diana herself – to my shock, for I cannot think of anyone more English than Diana – was born in Chicago. Hay is a town of travelers who stopped; it is where urbanites come to hide from their home cities and from the tentacles of big-city traders and publishers.

"The most important geographic feature of Hay," Booth likes to say, "is that it is *not near London.*"

But, for a few days every May, London draws itself awfully near indeed. The Hay Festival is now one of the world's largest literary events; all of a sudden the little streets are flooded with editors and the edited, and with BBC crews and autograph seekers, all chasing down dozens of writers of the day – Kazuo Ishiguro, Zadie Smith, Norman Mailer, Martin Amis, Beryl Bainbridge, and whoever else happens to get recognized from their book jacket photo and then cornered while buying dandruff shampoo at the Spar.

Back when it started in 1988, it was the Hay Literary Festival, and some writers still like to grumble that the later loss of *literary* is no accident; after all, the two biggest draws for next year's festival are likely to be Paul McCartney and Bill Clinton. But professional authors still rule the roost here, and most of the festival events are still sponsored by publishers or Hay booksellers. Still, not everyone is satisfied: there is always one notable figure absent from the festival.

"This is a town of secondhand books," Booth tells me one day as he watches me sort books. "Who benefits from a festival about new books? I can think only of one store in Hay that *might*."

"Who's that?"

Booth harrumphs and lights one of his sickly brown cigarettes; then it dawns on me: ah-*ha*. Now I understand why Diana Blunt might not be interested in buying his autobiography. I have only owned a copy of it a couple days myself, and it is a curious feeling to speak to the man during the day while reading *My Kingdom of Books* after work.

"Still," Booth says, "this is a great secret, but I may yet reach a truce with your landlady. I *might* join in next year's festival. But I have not decided."

Which is not to say that Booth has reached a truce with everybody else here. Once a town has forty booksellers, it becomes less likely that every one of them will get along, especially with a fellow who was one of the two living entries in a book titled *The World's Greatest Cranks and Crackpots*. (Once Keith Moon died, Booth became the book's *only* living entry.) There is a long-standing rivalry between Booth and a well-moneyed London entrepreneur, Leon Morelli. Booth's enterprises always seem to be one step ahead of the ground giving way beneath their feet, while Morelli's are almost grimly secure with funding. When Booth's Cinema Bookstore began to fail in the early eighties, Morelli bought it off him. Booth claims the fellow then wrenched the price down at the last moment and poached his best employees. Morelli became the president of the local Chamber of Commerce, and it was Morelli who, like a Monopoly player flush with goldenrod $500 bills, began buying up every property in sight from under the king of Hay's nose: the Swan Hotel, The Crown, Kilvert's, and the Corner Bookshop. Buyers began sniffing around Hay Castle itself.

The first observation of Morelli in Richard Booth's autobiography is that he has "gilded teeth," a sure sign of *villainy* in this land of horse-gummed gingivitis.

The saddest part of the whole rivalry is that Booth surely spends a great deal more time fulminating upon Leon Morelli than his foe ever spends thinking about him; for it is a privilege of power that you can ignore the people whom you are driving mad.

Before I had ever met Booth or heard of Morelli, I found a curious duality in the town of Hay. On one side of the castle hill was Booth's bookstore on Lion Street, a rambling monstrosity of half-opened shipping boxes, bindings ripped to shreds, of unguarded treasures left tossed in spiderwebbed corners. There are something like half a million books in this building – but nobody's really counting any more.

On the other side of the castle hill was the old former cinema, which Morelli had bought from Booth and restocked. The Cinema Bookshop is better run than Booth's: the hundreds of thousands of books here are priced and categorized, and related subjects are in proximity to each other. A proper modern cash register is at the front of the store, and a magneto-whatever exit gate will shriek if you try to steal their stuff. They even have a Serious Bookseller in their midst: Francis Edwards has its offices on the second floor, just in case you feel like leaving your backpack at their front desk and then blowing a couple hundred pounds on a clean leatherbound 1857 copy of *Relinquiae Hearnianae.*

This edition of Thomas Hearn's diary is almost worth it, if only for this entry on *juvenile indeliquency:*

21 January 1721. I have been told that in the last great plague in London none that kept tobacconists shops in London had the plague. It is certain that smoaking was looked upon as a most excellent preservative. In so much, that even children were obliged to smoak. And I remember that I heard formerly Tom Rogers, who was the yeoman beadle, say, that when he was that year, when the plague raged, a school-boy at Eaton, all the boys of that school were obliged to smoak in the school every morning, and that he was never whipped so much in his life as he was one morning for not smoaking.

The Francis Edwards section of the store is crammed with these sorts of books: pristine, quirky, and ancient.

Yet I have never bought a book in the Cinema Bookshop.

Not one. The titles themselves are curiously inert. Booth's, in its wide-armed embrace of everything that avalanches upon it, has become a de facto library of the forgotten, with both everything you could want and everything that nobody could ever want. But the

Cinema Bookshop is a used-book store run as if it were a new-book store; all the books are correctly priced, and there are no shocking bargains here. There is no surer way than that to suck the fun out of bookhunting.

Martin Like has caught me out in the Bull Ring with an armload of moldering hardcovers.

"I-I've a new house for sale," he says. "Just came up this morning. As soon as I saw it, I thought of you. We haven't even the papers on it yet, but . . . but . . . if you like, I could show it to you. Today, even."

"Ahhh . . ." I hesitate and rebalance the wavering bookpile. "I'll . . . Well. I don't want to speak for Jennifer, but maybe next time we're by your office we can have a look."

"Right, of course, of course."

It's hopeless, of course, of course. But I haven't the heart to tell him. We haven't heard back from First House's agent, and our bid is far below what they're asking; and yet, in our heads, we already own the place. Jennifer has been sketching out the alterations to its interior.

"Why don't you come over later today?" Martin says hopefully. "And we'll go over there. It's on Hendre Mews. It's just two hundred yards from here."

"Sure, okay."

Martin is right.

Granted, the house on Hendre Mews is even smaller inside than First House, just 890 square feet for a three-bedroom house. In the United States that would barely accommodate a one-bedroom apartment. But at least we don't have to rip anything ugly out of this place; it is a charming old row house of rough-hewn wood, sea-grass matting, and new yellow-blue checkerboard flooring.

The backyard is huge.

There's a grassy area for Morgan, and then a path winds along past a big shed. I point at it and turn to Jennifer. "Your painting studio."

Jennifer nods and peers inside it through a window.

"There's more," Martin says.

Another winding path leads up to a plot of land with some grape vines.

"We've never had this much land." Jennifer inspects the vines. "Whose grapes are these, by the way?"

"Yours, of course."

"Wait. Where does the property end?"

"Those trees over there." He points about fifty yards into the distance.

We look at each other incredulously and laugh. *"Wow."*

Morgan is deliriously happy and running in circles around the lawn. At one corner, by the patio, is a little square planter filled with smooth marbly stones. These he painstakingly picks up and then drops over and over. Then he yelps happily and runs out on the grass again.

"This comes with the property too." Martin points out a long, narrow shed, about thirty by eight, filled with what appears to be Snuffy Smith's moonshining stills.

"That," I say triumphantly, "is where I will set up my drum kit."

"You can fit a whole band in there."

A chicken buc-caws across our path.

"Whose chicken is that?" I ask Martin.

"Oh, yours."

There is a second floor in the Booth back building; the stairway to it is marked STAFF ONLY, and though I am now staff, I don't feel it, so I haven't ventured up there. All I can see from down here are mounds of boxes and books, stretching back into darkness like the last frames of *Raiders of the Lost Ark*.

Another fellow walks in today, a teenager. He looks a little lost, like me, as he ventures up the stairs.

"Where's the light switch?" he yells down.

I shrug helplessly. "I'm new here myself."

"Ah, right. Cheers then."

I hear his steps stumble around above me, stuttering over boxes – *Oof. Fookin' 'ell* – until click, the lights come on. He then works steadily and wordlessly, as do I. He is above me and out of sight, but by the sound of it he is shoveling the snowdrifts of wood pulp from one side of the warehouse to the other, and occasionally – CRASH – there is an avalanche. And it is, really. The slow sifting, then a quick, thundering crash of books collapsing, and then – I swear to God – the after-sounds of pebbles dribbling down, fine dirt sifting out, and a cloud of dust billowing out in the shocked silence. I hear him hacking and coughing, probably wiping his eyes. So I know he's okay for now, at least. In thirty years, he'll have bookseller's lung.

He leaves after a while, replaced by a gregarious-looking fellow who bounds up the steps without seeing me. There is a clattering of sawhorses and wood, and then the *schick schick schick* of someone sawing away.

Booth's has an endless need for bookshelves. Most of the shelves, carefully designed so as to be "within easy reach of a five-foot-two woman," were built by a local character named Frank English, a three-time army deserter who chain-smoked Woodbines, chain-drank Whitbreads, and more or less introduced Richard Booth to the art of living in Hay. English began employment with Booth's parents as their gardener and was angrily charged with drunkenness by the elder Mrs. Booth after one lost evening when his bedroom caught fire.

"No, Mrs. Booth," he patiently explained. "I came home stone-cold sober, and when I got into it, *the bed was already on fire.*"

Whereupon Frank was out of a job with the parents, but was gladly offered a new job by the son. By the time he died, Frank English had constructed some twenty-five miles of shelving for Richard Booth.

Yet there is always another book, always the ceaseless flow, always the next container ship to arrive, always the need for more. And so now there is another carpenter on hand to take up English's duties. When he runs out of wood, the carpenter creaks down the old stairs to fetch more planks from his van. He stops when he sees me.

"You the new fellow?" He is, by the sound of it, an immigrant himself.

"Yes, yes."

"Ah." He walks away. "You're working in a madhouse, boy."

I laugh politely – ha! ha! – and then sneeze violently from the book dust filtering down through the floorboards over my head, a very fine and choking mist of paper.

"The only decent books," Booth is fond of telling people, "are those published before the invention of shiny covers."

This is a problem, as my own little book on noble failures needs a cover. Historically, dust jackets are a new concern for authors; you don't see them much before the 1920s. And *dust jacket* is a strange name for this contrivance, as if books had anything to fear from dust. If you store a book properly, standing up, then the jacket doesn't cover the one part of the book that is actually exposed to dust, which is the top of the pages. So a dust jacket is no such thing at all; it is really a sort of advertising wrapper, like the brown paper sheath on a Hershey's bar. On this wrapper goes the manufacturer's name, the ingredients – some blithering about unforgettable characters or gemlike prose or gripping narrative – and a brief summation of who does what to whom in our gripping, unforgettable, gemlike object.

There will also be blurbs – from the *Times* and its ilk if it is a big, successful book, and from the *Dispatch* and its ilk if it is an unsuccessful book. If it is a first printing, it will be from fellow writers and advance reviewers like *Publishers Weekly*. If it is a dog of a manuscript that no one can say anything nice about, then the blurbs will be culled from praise for the author's previous book.

There are no sumptuary laws in publishing, but there may as well be: not only can you judge a book by its cover, most customers have no choice but to judge it this way. In 1963, Harcourt Brace opened its own Manhattan bookstore, and each editor was required to spend two weeks clerking there to, as the *New York Times* put it, "bring editors in closer touch with the public." But, alas, "the main discovery has been disillusioning. Chance buyers of books do not read the carefully chosen descriptive matter on the inside of the dust jacket; they look at the front of the jacket and buy or pass on."

There is an implicit code that customers rely on. If a book cover has raised lettering, metallic lettering, or raised metallic lettering, then it is telling the reader: *Hello. I am an easy-to-read work on espionage, romance, a celebrity, and/or murder*. To readers who do not care for such things, this lettering tells them: *Hello. I am crap*. Such books can use only glossy paper for the jacket; Serious Books *can* use glossy finish as well, but it is *only* Serious Books that are allowed to use matte finish.

Diminutively sized paperbacks, like serial romances or westerns or dieting and astrology guides, are aimed at the uneducated. But diminutively sized hardcover books are aimed at the educated – excepting those that are very diminutive, which are religious books aimed at the uneducated – and unless they are in a highly rectangular format, in which case they are point-of-purchase books aimed at the somewhat-but-not-entirely educated. However, vertically rectangular diminutive softcover books, which tend to be pocket travel guides, are aimed at the educated. But horizontally rectangular diminutive soft-cover books – a genre pioneered by *Garfield Gains Weight* – are not.

Then there are the colors. Bright colors, and shiny colors, are necessary for the aforementioned books with raised lettering. Black will work too, but only if used to set off the bright and shiny colors. Because, remember, with the customer base in mind, the book will need to be a bright and shiny object. Conversely, a work of Serious Literature will have muted, tea-stained colors. Black is okay here too, but only if used to accentuate cool blues and grays and greens.

Woe and alas to any who transgress these laws. A number of reviewers railed against *The Bridges of Madison County* because it used the diminutive hardcover size and muted color scheme of, say, an Annie Dillard book – thus cruelly tricking readers of Serious Literature into *buying crap*. Not to be outdone, the Harvard University Press issued Walter Benjamin's opus *The Arcades Project* with gigantic raised metallic lettering. One can only imagine the disgust of blowhard fiftysomethings in bomber jackets as they slowly realized that the project they were reading about was a cultural analysis of nineteenth-century Parisian bourgeoisie – and not, say, a tale involving renegade Russian scientists and a mad general aboard a nuclear submarine.

Finally, on Serious Books and crap alike there will be a head shot of The Author sitting still while looking pensive or smiling faintly into the indeterminate distance – the one pose that has no existence in the author's actual daily life. The size of this photo will be in inverse proportion to the quality of the book. If this photo is rendered in color, it is not a Serious Book. If there is no author photo at all, then it is a Serious Book indeed – perhaps even a textbook.

If a color photo of the author occupies the entire front cover, the book is unequivocal crap.

But I do not know what my cover will look like. When I check my e-mail today, there is a note from Dave, who is designing the jacket – springing a question that I hardly expect.

What do you want on the cover?

It is the question that every author deserves to be asked, I suppose, but not one that every author can answer. I certainly can't – it's my first book, and I've never even had to think about covers before. But it's coming out in eight months, and my publisher needs a picture now to put in its catalog for booksellers. Only – a picture of what? It's a history of noble failures, about the rise and then complete fall into obscurity of thirteen entirely different people over hundreds of years – inventors, poets, physicists, painters. How do you illustrate that theme? With a picture of water running down the plughole? Maybe by making your book pear-shaped?

I walk a circuit around town, out to the old poorhouse, then to St Mary's, and then back down to the community center, waiting for inspiration. It doesn't happen. This is because any writer who waits for inspiration is being an ass. Inspiration is achieved in humans by effort, a pumping of thoracic bellows – you have to breathe for yourself. No one will breathe for you.

I need to expose myself to art. There is print dealer on Castle Street; he is the only man in Hay with a security camera in his store, so you can observe yourself entering the store in grainy low-resolution splendor, and this Magoo-camera watches me as I peruse old *Punch* illustrations and plates of nineteenth-century natural history. Prints can be a nasty business. Lesser dealers perpetually operate under the reasonable suspicion of having mutilated old books to acquire their product. Why sell an intact old folio of botanical drawings for £500 when you can slice out scores of plates, dry mount them on board, and then sell them to Mondeo-driving punters for £60 each?

"Can I help you?" the dealer says.

"To be honest," I tell him, "I don't know what I'm looking for yet."

This may not make any difference. There are plenty of items in this world that I *do* know I am looking for, and I have not found them yet either. You know what I'd really like? A book of spurious fossils. In 1922 Riccardo Nobili published a wonderfully titled book, *The Gentle Art of Faking;* in it, he demonstrates just how incredibly cruel paleontologists can be to each other, with the case of the hapless Dr. Louis Huber of Würzburg:

> In the year 1727 two doctors of the town prepared a surprise for Huber . . . They fabricated fossils of fantastic animals and the most impossible shells. The imitations were generally modelled in clay with the addition of a hardening substance . . . [and] represented ants and bees of the most heroic proportions, crabs of a new line and shape, etc. These were carefully buried in ground of suitable character where Dr. Huber had been seen to excavate . . . Having made several of these most incredible discoveries, Dr. Huber saw fit to publish a work, consisting of a hundred folios . . . [with] illustrations reproducing with extreme exactitude Dr. Louis Huber's fantastic antediluvian find.

Maddeningly, Nobili never gives the title of Huber's work. I have not been able to find it in any library, nor, for that matter, have I even been able to find any mention of a Louis Huber. Perhaps, true his title, Riccardo Nobili is gently faking us. Or maybe Huber and his works were X-Actoed out of existence by print dealers.

It is useless to fret. What you mean to find matters less than what you do find. If it were not for the elusive Louis Huber, I never would have discovered François Huber. He was a naturalist who in the early 1800s made immense strides in apiary science by inventing glass hives that allowed the bees to be observed at work. Huber never performed the actual observations, though; he left that to his wife and to his faithful servant Burnens. But this only served to increase his fame. Huber, you see, was completely blind.

Chapter Twelve
Is Crap That
Nobody Reads Any More

FIVE PEOPLE ARE working in the back building today, and three are named Paul. There's me, there's Paul the teen who shifts books around upstairs and creates landslides, and Paul the fiftyish, curly-haired fellow who specializes in sixteenth-century British history. The latter leans against a shelf and watches me work.

"Now what exactly is the *American* Renaissance?" he asks me.

I start to explain the 1850s and F. O. Matthiesen and his eyes brighten. "Harriet Beecher Stowe," he exclaims, "was my first serious sale! A hundred-pound copy of an early edition of *Uncle Tom's Cabin.*"

Young Paul discovers an ancient *Playboy,* Carter era, amidst one of the incoming boxes and shows it gleefully to Sean, who nods approvingly – *"Heh. Heh."* They are perusing a pictorial on Foreign Girls, and next to each picture is a little flag for the country she represents; here is a topless picture of a young Mexican woman who, we are informed, by day works in a bank. I can't help wondering, as I do whenever I see one of these old magazines, where and what she is now – ensconced in some sort of fully clothed, respectable middle-aged life, I suppose. Perhaps she has made it to Loan Manager by now.

"So, you're Canadian?" the elder Paul asks me.

"Me? No."

"Oh." He becomes flustered. Clearly he is normally able to peg an accent. "Michigan?"

"No."

"But you are an American?"

I stare blankly. Could I *be* any more American? Maybe if I wore a Stetson embroidered *USA,* with Coke cans and Big Mac wrappers dangling from the brim, I guess.

"Yes, I am an American."

It's unfair, really, winding him up like this. I've lived in about nine or ten states, in every part of the country, and my parents and my brother are British. Even I don't know where I'm from anymore.

"Sooo . . ." He trails off.

"California," I finally say.

"Ah."

California is America's default setting.

Booth comes rattling in, trailing a dead stub of a cigarillo. He starts pulling random books off the shelves that I have marked MODERN FICTION and SOUTHERN WRITING.

"This is the kind of stuff we need," he announces as he hands me a clutch of books. "We must change how the image of America is perceived, that it's not all just fast food and ugly hotel chains. *A better image for America,*" he repeats several times, like a mantra. "And you are the expert who will do it. We need the whole melting pot . . . *ca-hack* . . . Norwegian-American fiction. Irish-American essays. And the Jewish, we must have anything Jewish."

He says this as if he is enumerating inventory for the bread aisle of a grocer: we need white bread, whole-wheat, rye, sourdough, hot-dog buns . . .

Booth stops for a moment and holds an unoffending volume up to his thick glasses.

"And this, look at this. *Moscow 1979.* Nobody buys this crap. Not in a thousand years. I want you to go to the stuff that people want – London, Steinbeck, American Renaissance! And the rest – I don't know, box it up for the warehouse, label it, and maybe we can sell it to Les for a tenner."

So now that I am two shelves short of finishing the weeding and alphabetizing of the whole area, I am to tear it all down again.

Okay.

Richard goes upstairs, to address the Pauls and Stewart and Sean. *"We've got to remake this building!"* he bellows. "We've got a mess, and it's my fault. I am an anarchist. But this building *must* turn a profit."

And yet the great thing about Booth's is that it *is* full of stuff that won't sell in a thousand years. You need to keep your ratio of the utterly obscure and the instantly familiar in careful balance: have too much of one or the other, and bankruptcy or insipidness is sure to follow. You need some odd "worthless" books because, like bending back lines to a vanishing point in a painting, the vanishing recognizability of a few titles in your stock gives the whole selection an appearance of depth. And there really is no telling what people might actually want. Everyone has their own peculiar notions of value; one story among book traders is of a dealer who, upon asking a rural squire how much he'd sell his ancient family library for, was informed: *The price of a couple of bitches.*

Still, some titles truly are worthless, cannot even be given away. Among the many banes to a secondhand dealer's existence, four unloved genres reign supreme: textbooks, theology, celebrity autobiography, and military history.* Booth will do anything to get rid of these sort of volumes: at one point a chain-saw sculptor was allowed

---

* When I was in a Manhattan Barnes & Noble earlier this year, they had a table marked NONFICTION FOR FATHER'S DAY. Every single title was about war. The notion of masculinity among such booksellers is as pinched and narrow as the his-and-hers aisles of Hot Wheels and Barbies at a Toys "R" Us.

to use blocks of remaindered books to create a full-scale model of a Rolls-Royce. "When he power-sawed through one of my desks," Booth says, "I lost patience with patronizing the arts."

Unsalable books meet all sorts of grim fates in Booth's autobiography:

> Smartly-suited US evangelists and old television and radio presenters could expect certain death by fire in Hay . . . At one time I thought there might be a future in barter and offered to exchange books for the woodburning stoves that were very popular in the area. I did receive some eggs from a Sennybridge doctor, but to make the books properly combustible we needed a blower, or a log-machine to bind them tightly in wires.

Booth resorted to heaping up pyres of books in the field behind his castle, dousing them with petrol, and then setting them on fire. But book burning, useful though it is for purging copies of *Catcher in the Rye* and *The Color Purple,* was not well suited for large-scale literary extinction. Booth's castle holds a commanding hilltop position over the center of town, and the burning books there were whipped and wafted by updrafts of wind, tossing burning leaves of text up high over the forbidding castle walls and floating a ghostly rain of blackened pages onto the populace below.

As I leave Booth's, I linger for a moment in front of the small shop window next door. It is a new business, but of the strangest sort. You stand at the plate glass and look into what appears to be someone's living room: a table with some teacups arrayed upon it, an easy chair with a half-read newspaper, a side table with an old rotary telephone, and a few books arranged up on a shelf. It is like a cutaway view of a private and modest little house, the sort of scene you get in old cartoons when half a building collapses, and the other half continues showering and going about its chores, unwittingly exposed to your sight.

Only here, each item has a small price tag on it. There is an unmarked door by which you may go inside. I quietly turn the knob; it is unlocked. And yet I would no sooner enter this store than I would the house of a complete stranger. It feels too real, too strangely exposed, like a sort of Man Cage at the zoo.

The idea is not new. In 1924 David Garnett wrote a strange little book called *A Man in the Zoo;* its protagonist, one John Cromartie, notices a major omission in the Primate House at the London Zoo: there is no specimen of *Homo sapiens*. He obligingly offers himself up as an exhibit, a man in a glass-and-mesh cage who sits in an overstuffed chair reading Henry James novels, playing with a cat, and ignoring the gawking zoo visitors. The zoo puts a sign up on his cage:

> *Homo sapiens*
> MAN
> This specimen, born in Scotland,
> was presented to the Society
> by John Cromartie, Esq.
> Visitors are requested not to irritate the
> Man by personal remarks.

And yet this storefront is rendered even stranger by its absence of any people at all. It is as still as a museum diorama. I have never seen a customer in there. Nor, come to think of it, have I ever seen an employee.

"Explain this to me again?"

We are sitting in Martin Like's office, with the tax map of Hay spread out before us. The town is cut up into little parcels and buildings, and I look at it and marvel: I didn't know what a dense patchwork this town's land holdings were.

"Hendre Mews will accept your offer," Martin repeats. "But on one condition. If you sell this land out back at some future date, they want half."

"Half of the land?"

"No. Half of the *money*."

Jennifer and I look at each other, mystified.

"Martin," she finally says, "are they selling this property or not?"

"Yes, yes." He reddens slightly. "Indeed they are. I understand your concern. But it should not be a difficulty."

"So they are selling it . . . but they are not *really* selling it."

"Oh, no," he insists. "They are selling it."

Hmm.

"And if we put the property up for sale someday . . ."

"Y-yes?"

"Will this condition be binding on the next owner as well?"

"For ten years, yes."

There is a long, heavy silence in the room.

"Martin, nobody's going to buy it."

"I-I don't think . . . you see, it's possible to make . . . ," he stammers. "Well, let me explain."

And he does explain; he has to, because he is representing the seller and is bound to them, no matter how sensible he is and how delusional they are.

After we leave the office and push our stroller back down the street, Jennifer lets loose a long sigh.

"I wish we could buy a house from Martin. He's such a nice guy, and we put him to so much trouble."

We pass by Kilvert's, and its sign creaks a little in the breeze. Now it is my turn to let out a long sigh. "How does anybody find a place to live in this country?"

Jennifer has been working steadily, for about a month now, on needlepoint. But not just any needlepoint. She does not work from a pattern. Or rather, she does, but it is an exceedingly complex mathematical formula for the number and color of the stitches, the slight variation of which results in total restructuring, a different sum you might say; it is an abstract needlepoint. It is not so much a representational needlepoint as a mathematical equation rendered in yarn. Even people who can't sew are liable to engage themselves thus; Hobbes was so fascinated by geometry that, when lolling about in bed, he would take to drawing lines and diagrams on his thighs and on the bedsheets.

We are ensconced back in our apartment, Morgan is asleep, I am staring at the ceiling, and Jennifer is stitching. *World Report* mumbles drowsily from the kitchen.

"You look perturbed."

"Mmm?"

"Perturbed." Stitch. "You look perturbed."

"Oh, I'm thinking."

Inevitably: "About?"

"The cover of my book."

"I thought you'd be thinking about the house falling through."

"Oh. That too."

"So the design we sent to Dave . . . ?"

This was a sort of phrenological head with a paste-in of a nightmarish Hogarth study that I had found over at the print shop.

"He doesn't like it. He said a phrenological head will make it look like a how-to book on improving your memory."

Jennifer pauses to calculate. Stitch. "So you need a new design?"

"Yeah."

"Honey, maybe you should go to Booth's."

"Booth's? I just got away from Booth's."

"I'm just saying. You might get an idea there."

"I suppose."

I mope my way over to Booth's and look around the endless dusty aisles. Look at all these dead shelves. For every book you recognize there are twenty that you don't. Usually this heartens me – what an adventure to read those twenty! But now I just feel kind of blue about it. Even writing and publishing a bad book, a boring and stupid book, takes gargantuan effort. And for what? For this? For some elderly anarchist to burn your remains in a back lot?

For a writer with a book coming to press, to work here – why? It is like a pregnant woman taking a job at the morgue. You stare oblivion in the face every day in a store like this. There is a critical trajectory to most books and their writers. Your first book is "promising"; then your second is "a disappointment"; your third and onward are "competent."* But what of the man who writes only a single book, or even two or three books, and then *disappears*, to not even occupy a single zero or one on any hard drive in the world? You can lift a book out of the fiction section – say, *Cabbage in the Grass,* a novel published in 1956 by Leopold Louth. A *New Statesman* review that year by Sean O'Faolain lauded him as "our most arresting humorist since Kingsley Amis, and of infinitely wider range and, I *think,* of a keener intelligence." And I imagine an urbane reader such as yourself has heard of Kingsley Amis.

But have you ever heard of Leopold Louth?

Where do the Leopold Louths of the world go? For *Cabbage in the*

---

* Please accept my apologies: this book is a disappointment.

Grass is indeed a good book. It tells the tale of one hapless Tolstoy-toting idealist, Rupert Barrener-Tapp, as he declines and falls from his ancestral manor into a series of disastrous attempts at working-class life, culminating in his becoming a repairman at the dawn of the television era, where he services the thirteen-inch black-and-white tellies of lonely housewives.

"Vertical hold!" coos one to him during a bit of rutting on the sofa.

Louth wrote three books in the 1950s, promising stuff in the Evelyn Waugh line of things, and then – poof! When I did online searches for his name, I had zero hits. *None:* not even a hit for some other guy with the same name. I even tried to reprint his book myself. I put in a letter at the *TLS,* I wrote his publisher, Victor Gollancz – or what is left of his publisher forty years later, chewed up and digested in mergers and consolidations – I e-mailed everyone in Britain that I could find named Karl Louth or Louis Louth, the two sons mentioned in his book's dedication. Nothing. Leopold Louth is gone.

I make my way to the back building, where my work for tomorrow lies in scattered and disordered piles. Still sitting atop one pile, where Booth tossed it, is the copy of *Moscow 1979* – the crap, as he says, that nobody reads any more.

So I read it.

I pull out a stool and sit down with the soiled little volume. And here's the funny thing for a 1979 tourist guide: its publication date is *1940.*

Moscow 1979, it turns out, is not a tourist guide at all: it is a guide to the future, or about what used to be the future. And the future is not, according to Erik and Christiane von Kuehnelt-Leddihn, a very happy place. For one thing, socialism has spread out from Russia and taken over most of the Western world – every country except Britain and the United States. In fact, Italians have embraced godless egalitarianism so enthusiastically that the pope is now Filipino, and the Vatican is located in San Francisco.

That's how you know that it's a dystopia, I suppose.

Moscow 1979 seems to be a sort of missing link between *Brave New World* and *1984*. The book's protagonist, Ulyan Karlovitch, blunders his way through this Socialist Paradise in his job at a plaster factory and inadvertently finds love at a coed state-run brothel, where normally the rooms are kept pitch-black for state-approved anonymity and equality in relieving one's urges. He soon finds himself becoming the widower father of a newborn:

Ulyan bent over the little aluminum cradle and contemplated the child . . . There it was; a little miracle with a beating heart. The metal plate over the cradle bore the number 31.317-C-XIII. This was an easy number to remember. A cheap color-print was hanging over the metal plate; it was a view of Leninsk, the center of the city, with skyscrapers, elevated trains, bridges and floodlights. But Ulyan only saw the number. Practically nothing but the number. Without giving the doctor another look, he left.

And so Ulyan leaves his child to cruel fate. Ulyan himself does not fare well at the book's end, either: after finding God in a godless land, he and a new love are sent praying down the conveyor belt of a human rendering factory, where an enzyme wash begins to separate the skin from their living bodies.

It is not well-written; the authors have An Important Point to Make, and that rarely bodes well for aesthetics. But it is not crap, even if nobody reads it any more. Erik von Kuehnelt-Leddihn fled from Austria as a young aristocrat in 1938, just ahead of the Führer's grasp; it's easy to see what was on his mind as he and his wife spent 1939 writing this vision of the future. He went on to become a Catholic theologian in the United States, writing cogently well into his nineties. I wonder whether, six decades later, anyone ever surprised him by asking about this book.

That is the curious and humbling thing about having written a book: as forgotten as it may become, it is frighteningly permanent and it will most certainly outlive you. Hawthorne tried to obliterate his first published novel, *Fanshawe,* by buying back and burning every single copy – even seizing copies given to friends and relatives. He never spoke of the book to anyone; his own wife did not learn of the novel's existence until after his death. Yet he did not succeed – a few copies slipped through his grasp. Hawthorne is dead; but *Fanshawe* now thrives in multiple editions. And no matter what else they did in or with their lives, no matter how many years and continents they spanned, Erik and Christiane von Kuehnelt-Leddihn will forever be the authors of *Moscow 1979.* When you publish a book, you know how at least one line of your obituary will someday read.

I toss *Moscow 1979* back down; the sun will be setting soon, and it's my turn to go home and watch Morgan now. I pass through the magazine section of the store on the way out, pausing to peruse an 1824 copy of *The Mirror of Literature, Amusement and Instruction;* it includes a series of articles on curious wills and testaments. To wit:

JOSEPH DALBY, late of the Parish of St. Mary-le-bone, proved July 27, 1784. I give to my daughter, Ann Spencer, a guinea for a ring, or any other bauble she may like better, I give to her lout the husband one penny to buy him a lark-whistle, I also give to her said husband of redoubtable memory, my --- hole for a covering to his lark-whistle, to prevent the abrasion of his lips, and this legacy I give as a mark of my approbation of his prowess and nice honour, in drawing his sword on me at my own table, naked and unarmed as I was, and he well fortified with custard.

The British, you understand, feel rather strongly about their custard – and also, apparently, about their lark-whistles.

Under this magazine lies an old and dirty print, folded over and ratty. I open it slowly, reading the caption at the bottom first as it unfolds. It is a reprint of a 1660 map of the solar system by Andreas Cellarius, and a weakly inked one at that, quite useless. But as I open it fully, there it is, *there it is:*

My book cover.

Chapter Thirteen
Views the Damaged Past

DIANA IS PLACING newly arrived copies of a Margaret Atwood novel on display in Pemberton's, carefully arranging them; in the back, Morgan is carefully deranging the entire children's shelf.

"I don't see why you two are so set on an old house," she says.

"We want something nice," Jennifer pleads.

"Warren Close is a perfectly good neighborhood."

"We're from a country of Warren Closes. We want something old."

"You have an old house yourself, Diana." I gesture about us. "It's got all these hardwood floors and plaster, and old beams. You know how it is."

"Indeed I do know how it is," she says dryly. "Your wiring goes out and your basement floods. What's so wonderful about an old house with beams? Buy a new house and toss a beam in it."

She pauses and looks at us. It is clear that we are a hopeless pair.

"I suppose I shan't dissuade you," she continues. "If you really want something nice, you need to go out to Cusop Dingle."

She says this *Kew-sup,* which I have to remember. This is one of the easier place names to remember, though all the Welsh names here throw me; I still mispronounce our town's Welsh name of Y Gelli. Welsh is a form of cipher, like German Enigma machines –

none of the letters is pronounced the same as the letter would indicate to an English speaker, but is instead moved one over – thus an *L* is pronounced *K*, an *F* is an *E*, and an *A* is . . . whatever letter comes before *A*. Some sort of choking sound.

Hazel hauls over another sliced-open publisher's shipping box to her.

"Cusop Dingle," Diana adds, "is the Beverly Hills of Hay."

"Yes. I can tell from the name."

And so we load Morgan into his stroller and walk out past the Bull Ring, past the grotty little Laundromat, and past the bank. As you cross the edge of town, the fields stretch away into the far distance, and there are lots of green paddocks and burbly creeks. Every other driveway winds off in the distance to some pretty little B&B homestead.

"Look!" Jennifer points at a field. "Morgan, look!"

A flock of sheep are gazing up and taking notice of us. I can always see these sheep from our apartment's bathroom, for its window looks out to fields dotted with white fluff. Now the fluff has faces and legs: they are no longer an abstraction.

"Baa!" yells Morgan, bouncing frantically in his stroller.

A sheep ambles over to the fence; Morgan desperately wants to reach down and pet it. But – poor thing – the sheep has open sores on his head. Flies buzz about it. I am beginning to understand the appeal of a vegetarian diet. I hold Morgan at a safe distance.

"Sheep! Sheep!" I tell him cheerfully, as I cringe at the friendly injured creature.

We walk onward to Cusop Dingle. This is where Booth and most of the other town burghers live. The farther you walk along, the prettier and stonier the cottages become; they are soon surrounded by walls drowning in ivy, and remind me of the old parts of town back in Princeton and Amherst. It is the look of respectable money.

Three kids in baggy pants and skate gear pass us in the lane. Skate rats in the Welsh countryside? Their source turns out to be a now emptied local playground, a fine one with swings and a slide. We let Morgan loose to run around in dizzying circles on the grass. At a house on one side of the park, a woman and her teenage son are clearing brush from the backyard. Jennifer ventures up to talk with them.

"Hi. Nice day to be outside."

"'Tis. You know," says the woman, "you're the first person to talk to us all week."

"Oh?"

"We just had a funeral."

"I'm . . . I'm really sorry to hear that."

"Oh" – the woman shrugs helplessly – "neighbors have been steering clear. That's how it is."

Everyone has been respectfully avoiding the grieving household – when, as usual, all they want is some semblance of normalcy. Two dogs caper among the brush, merrily getting in the way.

"Off! Off, you." She shoos one aside.

The area, she says, has been changing; people are moving in and buying and expanding the old houses.

Jennifer points back toward Hay. "We've already seen two places being renovated on this street, just walking up here."

"It's people from London. And abroad." The woman smiles.

"You don't say?"

"You go further up that road" – she nods – "and the houses get even nicer."

Not everyone agrees that the nicer houses are a good thing. If you look closely at the bookstore cashier desk in Hay Castle, you will see a neglected old pile of the complete works of none other than Richard

Booth himself: bumper stickers for the Kingdom of Hay, a 45 rpm single of *The King of Hay's Greatest Hits,* a Hay passport bearing the legend "His Majesty's Secretary of State Phillip Macdonough will protect, in pubs, any person holding a Hay passport and too many drinks." But most of all, there is pamphlet after pamphlet penned by Booth, bearing titles like:

Abolish the Wales Tourist Board
God Save Us from the Development Board for Rural Wales
Bring Back Horses
Why Woolworth Will Destroy Brecon
An Address by the King of Hay

Nestled among these is a thick, green paperbound booklet, the most inconspicuous and quaintly titled of the lot:

Bureaucracy in Brecon and Radnor:
with reference to a horse ride through Cusop Dingle

It is, I think, one of the most mournful little booklets that I have ever seen. I do not mean simply in its form, which is like any inexpensive, locally printed effort typed up on a Selectric; no, it is the contents and tone of the book. Here is how it begins:

About a mile outside the town of Hay-on-Wye in Breconshire, lies the town of Cusop Dingle, an area only reachable by horse. The motor road finishes a mile outside of town but eight bridle ways lead up into twenty miles of some of the most spectacular scenery in the British Isles. The horse economy was successful here, four hundred people lived and worked in this town producing goods for the town of Hay. With the introduction of the tractor economy the community failed. The population sank to less than twenty and a few hundred sheep . . . what happened?

What follows is a sort of illustrated courtroom exhibit showing the unraveling of a local economy of pig farmers, apple orchards, and quarries; there is page after page of photographs of disused bridle paths, ragged wire fencing, crumbling stone walls, and skeletal barns. The caption beneath one picture of a collapsed lime kiln reads: "The Brick & Slate maker of the Dingle suicided when his living was destroyed."

Booth reserves special scorn for the Forestry Commission and its "University jobs," and for the cheesy efforts of the Wales Tourist Board. But he also takes a few digs at "weekenders" and other outsiders who buy up old schools and almshouses and renovate them into modern living quarters, usually while trampling on the locals and fencing off public rights-of-way. It all makes for sad, gloomy reading. A visitor like me sees nothing but quaintness in Hay, and a certain stark beauty in ruins; but a longtime resident sees . . . well, ruin. And yet to harangue against their renovation seems hopeless too. Decay might be the best growth industry left in Wales. The damaged past, artfully reused, is all most of us ever have to work with anyway.

More than anything else, though, Hay is full of damaged *books*. To get them fixed you have to go to the local bookbinder, and there are two in this village. Both are named Christine. Christine Cleaton works in the old blacksmith's shop next to the Black Lion pub; it is just under street level, so you crouch a little and peek through the ancient glass, then step down into the doorway. This is a fine opportunity, particularly after a pint next door, to cuff your head on the low entranceway.

This is what I do, more or less. Then I knock on the door.

"Come in." Christine motions and wanders back inside, seemingly oblivious to me again. I walk inside and look around her workshop; it feels immediately familiar. It takes me a moment to figure out why.

It looks precisely like my father-in-law's lute workshop in Sonoma County. Outside *his* place is a vast panorama of hot sunlight blazing down on leaning sheds, fallow yellowed fields, and distant dots of grazing cattle. Inside – stacks of painstakingly collected rare woods, file folders stuffed with wrinkled sheet music, racks of handmade templates of lutes, violins, krummhorns. Upstairs, by a disused shower where he hangs varnished instruments to dry, there is a table jumbled with ancient glass jars of translucent brown, red, and golden liquids. They fight for table space with an ever-increasing pile of empty diet Dr Pepper cans, and a battered boom box with a few smudgy old folk tapes.

Christine's workshop looks exactly the same, except the cattle grazing outside are book tourists, the hot sunlight is cold drizzle, the sheet music is marbled paper, the lute racks are book presses crunching down old copies of Macaulay, the ancient glass jars are filled with rabbit glue and deionized water, and the diet Dr Pepper cans are cups of tea. Come to think of it, the only thing that is precisely the same is the battered boom box and the smudgy folk tapes.

And yet it *feels* the same. It is the clutter, the worn wooden handles of old tools and darkened brown of old cast iron, the dripped-out cans and jars, the mysterious little drawers of bits and pieces, half hanging out to reveal their contents; the light filtered through a dirty window. Books are piled up here and there, everywhere; octavos, quartos, folios. Most of them are missing spines or the boards are detached. I gingerly touch one mutilated folio.

"How does this happen?" I finally ask.

She looks up from her stitching. "Use. The boards, the hinges, and the cover, those are the only moving parts in books. And eventually they will fall off."

"But" – I nod at the splayed guts of the volume before me – "nobody reads a book *this* much."

"Well, it's the quality of the material too." She stops stitching. She has had to explain this before. "When you had a growing middle class in the late nineteenth and early twentieth century, and better transport, you had a demand for more books, more magazines . . . more everything. And that meant coming up with the same kind of materials – bindings, thread, leather – in much greater quantities and much faster. And so they had to cut corners. Here, look at this book."

She passes me an octavo casualty.

"They used a cheap hide, and tanned it poorly," she continues. "Sooner or later, you pay for that. These books were never intended to last this long. I don't know if the publishers really thought about it."

"You get a lot of books like this?"

"Some. Sometimes you just get a clothbound book, and they want you to reattach a cover. And that's not hard, maybe fifteen pounds. Maybe thirty or thirty-five for leather bindings. But a book like that folio, when you're having to restitch the spine and reattach boards, then a big job like that can run twenty, thirty hours or more. That becomes expensive."

I look more closely at the folio. It appears to be a Napoleonic history, though I'm not sure. The spine has torn away like a dry husk, and the pages are so frail that I'm afraid to even lift up the endpapers.

"You can fix this?"

"Oh, of course. Some can't be fixed. Most books can, as long as you are willing to pay for it. But books that were cheaply made and are of not enough interest today, when they get into such bad repair – well,

I suppose they get binned, don't they? They never even make it here."

It takes about ten years for a load of books to be digested by Hay, she says. When a flood of library books came in about twenty years ago, it was a decade before she stopped seeing them around town. Christine's been binding for twenty-five years now; and so during that time at least two or three full cycles of books have passed through town to be sold or . . . *binned*.

It is a strange thought to have in room of woeful-looking books: these are the lucky ones.

I look back upon the bookbinder's as I walk away and muse. Bookbinding has changed so little over the years that a binder waking from a century-long sleep could walk into Christine's shop and immediately get to work. There have been some innovations, but fewer than you might think. You can resize paper now with a pulp-based goop called Methocel, though the stuff has a far more common use: as the thickener in fast-food milk shakes. Methocel – or hydroxypropyl methylcellulose, as we used to call it in my grandma's kitchen – is also used in tile grout and plywood laminate; and if you've ever struggled to suck a fast-food milk shake through a straw, this fact will not surprise you. I think our ancient binder would be more confounded by the milk shake, though, than by the resizing process. And progress has crept only a little into the spines of books, such as the use of polyester thread in postwar bindings; in fact, the downfall of Konrad Kujau's infamous "Hitler diaries" in the 1980s was the anachronistic presence of polyester in the binding.

Long before those ill-fated diaries, Edmund Pearson published his wonderful 1920 book *Books in Black or Red*. I have read it many times over now; it may be one of the most pleasant books for any bibliophile to own. Pearson reveals a truism hiding in plain sight:

forgeries fail because they attract attention to themselves. Currency counterfeiters, for example, never forge five-dollar bills out of bleached one-dollar bills, despite the respectable 400 percent return this would yield; they go for higher denominations, which are precisely the ones that get scrutinized. If you forged something *modest,* no one would look closely enough at it to know.

Pearson opens his meditation upon forgery with one reader's memorable reaction to Montgomery Carmichael's biography *The Life of John William Walshe:*

> "I have heard," said a Churchman of some rank – I think he was a Dean or an Archdeacon, for I remember that he reminded me of Trollope – "*I have heard* that that book is really *fictitious* from beginning to end!"
>
> And he glared at me as if he intended to follow his remark with a medieval curse. I told him that I had heard the same thing and from good authority.
>
> "Well!" he said, pounding the table, "the man who would do that is a hound! An absolute *hound!*"

What is so beautiful about the biography of Walshe is that it is *utterly unremarkable:* it recounts the uneventful scholarly life of a pious English expatriate in Italy, and as Pearson puts it, "It contained not one atom of satire." The book is a senseless and motiveless act of forgery, which renders it almost perfectly immune to suspicion. Had it not been for an alert reader who discovered Walshe's nonexistence, it would have passed into an infinitesimally small but secure corner of history, amusing no one but its author. And, in fact, he *does* succeed at times: if you go to Alibris, for example, you will find this book still listed as a biography of "one of the foremost Franciscan scholars of the time."

Most forgers lack Carmichael's restraint or his philosophical detachment from motive. They must forge big *salable* things. And, admittedly, Hitler does seem like the perfect target for profitable fraud: after all, it is unlikely that his estate will sue you. My favorite concoction, though, occurred before Der Führer's death: Pauline Kohler's 1940 memoir *I Was Hitler's Maid*. Surely that title alone deserves some sort of literary immortality. Kohler, having escaped from employment at his Berchtesgaden residence, blurted out to the British public in 1940 all the details of Hitler's personal life – what time he got up, what he ate for breakfast, and most importantly, an array of sexual acts that can only be described with the aid of a slide whistle. *I Was Hitler's Maid* also provides crucial insight into the mind of a world leader with this quotation:

> I never feel tired when my Storm Troopers and soldiers march
> past me and I stand at the salute. I never move. My arm is as if
> of granite – rigid and unbending. But Goering can't stand it. He
> has to drop his arm after half-an-hour of salute. He's flabby. But
> I am hard. For two hours I can keep my arm stretched out in
> the salute. That is four times as long as Goering. That means
> that I am four times stronger than Goering. It is an amazing
> feat. I marvel at my own power.

Sadly, Kohler does not provide further details on which boy in the German High Command can spit the farthest, belch the loudest, or most accurately write his name in the snow. And I guess now we'll really never know, because *I Was Hitler's Maid* was exposed in 1970 as a profitable hoax perpetrated by two unemployed journalists. One of them explained that he and his fellow hack had been operating "under the stimulus" of a substantial number of Canadian whiskeys. It took them two weeks to write and sold ten thousand copies.

For sheer idiotic chutzpah, though, it would be hard to top Patience Worth. Her name is forgotten today, but at one time she – or her spirit, at least – was very famous indeed. In 1916 Henry Holt and Company published Caspar Yost's "discovery" of a new poet and novelist; or rather, of a very old poet and novelist. Communicating through the Ouija board of a St. Louis housewife was the spirit of Patience Worth, a Puritan woman filled with so much poetry, so much homily, and so much family drama that she was a veritable Oprah's Book Club in spirit form.

In introducing her, Yost gives us this weird amalgam of Tonto and Ren-Faire geek:

> The pointer suddenly became endowed with an unusual agility, and with great rapidity presented this introduction:
> "Many moons ago I lived. Again I come. Patience Worth my name."
> The women gazed, round-eyed, at each other and the board continued:
> "Wait. I would speak with thee. If thou shalt live, then so shall I. I make my bread by thy hearth. Good friends, let us be merrie. The time for work is past. Let the tabbie drowse and blink her wisdom to the firelog."

I suspect that Mr. Yost was also enjoying a substantial number of *stimulating* Canadian whiskeys, and a good laugh, as he wrote this. One can only imagine his surprise when, from this inauspicious start, there arose a Patience Worth industry in the 1920s – a series of novels and poems written via Ouija board by the good Mistress Worth, a Patience Worth magazine, even a Patience Worth Publishing Company. People *believed* it – even, amazingly, after Patience Worth wrote a Victorian family melodrama. Considering that neither

Victorians nor novels had existed in Worth's day, this was an impressive achievement indeed.

A few spoilsports finally tried to find Patience Worth's birth and death records. But Yost was careful not to reveal her precise birthplace or era; Patience, he said, had never imparted this information. And so, too, the existence of a Patience Worth gravesite was never established. I think we can be reasonably sure, though, of the existence of a sizable Caspar Yost checking account.

Yost rightly sensed that many people are partial to the notion that, like St. Louis housewives with a Ouija board, all writers are somehow mere vessels for Truth and Beauty when they compose. That we are not really in *control*. This is a variation on that twee little fable that writers like to pass off on gullible readers, that a character can develop a will of his own and "take over a book." This makes writing sound supernatural and mysterious, like *possession by the faeries*. The reality tends to involve a spare room, a pirated copy of MS Word, and a table bought on sale at Target. A character can no more take over your novel than an eggplant and a jar of cumin can take over your kitchen.

Still, readers of Yost's little farrago did have the opportunity to discover a fine new poetic talent. Not Patience Worth's. Printed in the back of the book, amidst ads for *Mason's Hypnotism and Suggestion* and *Telepathy and the Subliminal Self,* was a notice for the forthcoming volume by a "new American poet." His name was Robert Frost.

Dobson has come out to glare at me. He may be Booth's longest-serving employee now, and I've seen him around the store for years – always dressed in a fawn-colored anorak and noiselessly haunting the second floor. But I've never really spoken with him. Presumably Booth has just lectured him, as he has everyone else here, on how I am *the new expert in American literature.*

"Who are you?" he demands.

"Oh, hi!" I offer to shake hands. "I'm Paul."

He says nothing.

"Richard asked me to sort through these books," I continue. "American literature."

"*I* handle American literature. In the other building."

Dobson watches in silence as I weed the shelf to Booth's new specifications. Then, carefully choosing, he cherry-picks what I've left behind.

"Ah, yes," – he grabs a stack of Steinbeck – "we always need Steinbeck." *Snatch*. "And Mailer." *Snatch*. "And Whitman."

"Oh. Okay."

"You're American."

"Yes."

"My name," he says evenly, "is Dobson. And I have been working here" – he leans in, as if to wave a citation under my nose – *"for thirty-one years."*

And then he stalks off.

I feel a little ashamed of myself. Why shouldn't he dislike me? This store has been his refuge and much of his life's work. I have no intention of poaching upon his territory; I lack a serious interest in taking up bookselling as a career. He can keep the Whitmans and the Mailers; he can even have all of my Mary Johnstons. In fact, I wish he *would* have them.

The book trade does provide a certain shelter for those whose humors might ill-suit them for work elsewhere. I bought my 1920 copy of Morley's *The Haunted Bookshop* in Renaissance Books, a creaky old warehouse in Milwaukee; this store may be the closest thing the United States has to Booth's. The sullen clerk there did not return my greetings or my farewell, did not say a word, and did not show a single facial expression except irritation that I had interrupted his customerless routine. What this routine actually consisted of I can only guess, though by his countenance, I seem to have caught him halfway into sucking through a bagful of lemons.

Every city has such booksellers. Near my old digs in the Haight is a firetrap overflowing with unbelievably toppling piles of books, all slightly overpriced. Newcomers are halted in their tracks by the sight of these aisles of precarious piles and instinctively reach for the camera in their jacket. But in front of the store are two hand-lettered signs. The first reads:

> No Taking Photographs
> Inside of This Bookstore

And just below this, the second sign:

> No Asking Why You Can't
> Take Photographs

The signs are quite whimsical – at least, they are until you meet the stern visage of the store's owner.

I feel a hard little cramp of hunger in my gut, so I slip out of the fire exit of Booth's. I've no particular destination in mind, and I wander the blocks in the unfocused way that I get when I am too hungry.

I pause before Oscar's Bistro. It's an old building across the street from Pemberton's and just off the Bull Ring. Our apartment looks down into it, and I've passed by it many times, but for some reason I've never gone in. Whenever you move to a new town you develop a certain inertia; you cling to the few stores and spots that you happen to initially encounter in those first few confusing days of wandering the streets. By chance, we hadn't eaten in Oscar's in those first days here, but instead down the street in The Granary. We have stubbornly dined there ever since.

There is shepherd's pie in the window, and lamb with mint sauce, and ratatouille, and thick chewy bread, and . . . I walk inside.

Oscar's is crowded with tourists and locals alike. Plates are clattering and knives scraping. I ponder the shepherd's pie, then grab myself a tray and silverware. It is indeed very good shepherd's pie. But for once in my life, I haven't a newspaper to read while I eat, and so I watch my fellow diners instead. They are surprisingly dainty in the way they handle their food.

"On the Continent people have good food," the writer George Mikes once observed. "In England people have good table manners."

The notion that British food is not good is now the staple of a thousand tired travelogues. But it's simply not true any more. Britain spent a shocking portion of the last century either engaged in or recovering from wars; rationing persisted here through the 1950s. It is difficult to develop a modern cuisine out of ration cards; when food is dear and the winters are cold and wet, toast fried in pan drippings begins to make sense.

Actually, at one time toast really *was* a brilliant notion. It is beyond comprehension that someone had to invent toast, but I think the British may have done it. Witness this entry by a German traveler, Karl Moritz, as he passed through London in June 1782:

The slices of bread and butter, which they give you with your tea, are as thin as poppy-leaves. But there is another kind of bread and butter, usually eaten with tea, which is toasted by the fire and is incomparably good. You take one slice after the other and hold it to the fire on a fork till the butter is melted, so that it penetrates a number of slices at once: this is called *Toast*.

That toast seems to have eluded Germany for so long is mystifying; but then again, the Mayans never figured out how to use the wheel.

For all its past culinary failings, Britain has great food these days, and not just in the restaurants. Sandwiches, now mercifully free of butter and of the dreaded salad cream, have become the country's cheap meal of choice, and for good reason. British sandwich technology – there is such a thing, isn't there? – now puts other countries to shame. Sweet corn and tuna! Branston pickle and cheddar! Tikka chicken! And don't get me started on the existence of Indian food in the frozen aisle. For those with an actual inclination to perform work in the kitchen, cooking shows are flourishing on television and radio and are no longer limited to – as I saw on one such show a few years ago – explaining the recipe for *lemonade*.

That said, I will admit this much: to the American eye, the British have a curious relationship with their knives and forks. They hold their silverware wrong. The fork is held upside down, for spearing rather than scooping. Food is knifed mercilessly by the right hand while the downturned left hand pins the morsel down. You do not have to change hands to cut the food and then change hands back again before eating it; everything is instead performed in a single step with a minimum of wasted motion; there are none of the gentle inefficiencies of American cutlery usage.

To counterbalance their ruthless efficiency, the British developed table manners. They take them seriously. My elderly aunt, on her first overseas visit to America, indignantly marched out of a McDonald's after they refused to give her a knife and fork for her French fries.

"Aunt Kay," I pleaded as I was dragged away from my Happy Meal, "it's *McDonald's*. They don't *have* knives and forks."

"Bloody cheek," she muttered.

It got worse; the insistence of my British parents and brother on table manners caused all sorts of problems in our adopted homeland.

When I was a child in Perkiomenville, we had a neighbor who wielded an iron pipe to chase my older brother, Peter, a great distance – and in dead earnest – because he'd had the temerity to teach her children table manners. The sudden eruption of *please* and *thank you* and *Could I trouble you for* at her table drove her to even greater than usual madness, being as it was a distraction from her important project of stuffing hundreds of emptied True cigarettes packages into the wall cavities of her house. My brother's involuntary five-hundred-yard dash was much laughed at around our table, because the woman was simply a sad but amusing rural loon – at least, she was amusing until another neighbor's house mysteriously caught fire. We didn't see her around much after that.

I struggled hard for years to shake myself of the burden of table politeness – of a system where every request is made in the form of a complete sentence with several dependent clauses. Americans give you a queer look when you repeatedly do this over an entire meal. Our table manners are perfunctory: "Pass the ketchup?" It is an abbreviation of politeness, and you will no sooner hear it in some British homes than you will go *thru* anything in their country.

I loll about for a while over a cup of tea and then, fully sated, finally drag myself up out of my hard wooden chair. I do not feel like walking very far on this full of a stomach, so I turn immediately to the nearest bookseller; this being Hay, there is one adjoining Oscar's Bistro.

This shop, Mark Westwood Books, vies with Addyman Books as one of my favorite stores in Hay. It is not large, but it has a discernible taste behind its selections of old biographies, science texts, and medical journals. Here is a 1921 volume titled *Creative Chemistry,* which wisely advises us that "a man can live in a boiler factory, or in a cubist art gallery, but he cannot live in a room containing hydrogen sulphide." A set of the *London Medical Gazette* is crammed onto a basement shelf; one issue from 1844 debates the merits of medical marijuana. ("It is unfortunate, but true," laments one Dr. Ley, "that the Gunjah was deteriorated by age in this case, before it was appropriated for use as medicine.") Down in this low basement my eye is guided over to a large, faded-green volume: *The San Francisco Calamity by Earthquake and Fire,* by Charles Morris. Its cover is a drawing of a tall building collapsing into sheets of flame.

Even a hundred years ago, writers raced each other to make quick bucks off of cataclysms. The inscription inside this copy of *The San Francisco Calamity* reads, "To Mother – From Charlie + Emily – Winnipeg Canada – Oct 1906." The earthquake happened in April that year, so it must have been a rush job indeed to slap together a book of over four hundred pages and nearly a hundred plate photographs. Rushed as it must have been, the book is viscerally affecting in a way that no later account could be. It is there. And it is horrible: we hear of a man who threw himself onto the body of "his dead mother" in grief, until a soldier noticed that he was actually chewing her ears off between sobs, the better to get at her diamond earrings. *"Here is where you get what is coming to you,* said one of the soldiers, and with that he put a bullet through the ghoul. The diamonds were found in the man's mouth afterward." We see a soldier arguing with a local policeman and then gunning him down; and still other soldiers watching help-lessly as three men are trapped on top of the burning Hotel Windsor at Fifth and Market: "Rather than see the crazed men fall in with the roof and be roasted alive, the military officer directed his men to shoot them, which they did in the presence of 5,000 people."

The accounts of residents fleeing the burning city are less grue-some, but rather more surreal:

An observer tells of these incidents of the flight: "I saw one big fat man walking up Market Street, carrying a huge bird cage, and the cage was empty. He seemed to enjoy looking at the wrecked buildings. Another man was leading a huge Newfoundland dog and carrying a kitten in his arms. He kept talking to the kitten." Another observer says that he saw a lone woman patiently pushing an upright piano along the pavement a few inches at a time . . . the poor soul's one great treasure on earth.

Much of the book is filler. The publisher crammed accounts of other famous earthquakes along with every possible picture of San Francisco on hand, regardless of whether they had much to do with the earthquake. But I bet *The San Francisco Calamity* sold well nonetheless.

And this is why writers are thrust into the death trade – it is a secure profession, a thriving perennial business. In earlier centuries, one of the most common requests to printers was the production of elegies and essays upon the departed. When Thomas Chatterton once wrote an essay for a newspaper, he found its publication pushed aside by the unexpected death of the lord mayor. But with all the funereal hackwork this generated for him, he came out ahead. Or, as he put it in a note that he scratched down to himself:

			£.	s.	d.
Lost by his death in this Essay			1	11	6
Gained in Elegies	£2	2			
- - - - - - in Essays	3	3			
			5	5	0
Am glad he is dead by			£3	13	4

Chapter Fourteen
Is Awfully Late to Be
Introducing the Title Setting

TODAY IS MY last day working at Booth's. It is also payday, a Friday. The back room is dead quiet; I quickly perform a desperate mop-up operation, taking the jumbled boxes and stacks left and putting them into slightly less jumbled shelves.

An 1889 copy of Willis Johnson's *History of the Johnstown Flood*? Surely that goes in the Pennsylvania section. But then I discover another shelf, crammed in the back of the building: DISASTERS – U.S. I am stymied by the piles of books blocking the shelves I need to get to and finally just cram books down behind the mounds of books, hoping they'll somehow miraculously land on the right shelf. At least they're in the right part of the room. I think.

It gets more and more pointless. I start tossing books in the discard pile simply because they lack prices inside the cover. This place is meant to be chaotic. It cannot be anything else, as it exceeds the patience of ten men. I see it now – Richard has taken me out here, handed me a shovel, and left me in an Augean stable. And indeed there is a persistent odor in one section of the building, impregnating the U.S. Military section, and it is a distinctly male BO, like the steam-table water from a hot dog cart. I keep expecting to find the mummified body of a hapless customer under a collapsed stack of Pershing's memoirs, or maybe a sleepy hobo curled beneath a multivolume history of the War of 1812. But no – I am alone.

At quarter to five, as knocking-off time nears, I trudge up the groany stairs to the office. The doors are ajar, but . . . nothing is on, no one is there. I clomp back down and find a young woman at the front register, who after weeks here is yet another staff member that I have never met before and don't know the name of.

"Where do I get paid?"

"Oh," she says sadly, "they left hours ago."

The managers, that is.

"You could try the pub," she adds.

Fellow employees prove to be thin upon the ground on a Friday afternoon. I finally give up and leave; outside, at the corner of Bear and Pavement, I see Dobson and Paul talking. Today, payday, Dobson looks happier than he has been all week – radiant, even.

We have one last hope for a home in Hay: Sixpence House.

We have shied away from the Sixpence before. It is a desanctified pub, huge and rambling and hundreds of years old, thumped down squarely into the middle of town. Everyone in town, it seems, knows about the Sixpence House. Here is what they know:

1. It is a dump.
2. Everyone who buys it tries to sell it again, except that
3. They can't sell it.

Corollary to this:

A. It has a cellar full of water, and, oh, yes,
B. It is a dump.

When we mention the place to Diana Blunt, she is horrified.

"The Sixpence? You'll be right next to another pub. All those yobs coming out, full of beer – I shouldn't like it. It will be dreadfully noisy."

Jen and I have a good laugh at this. We, who in the Haight had to install thick soundproof acrylic on Morgan's nursery windows to muffle the sound of winos barfing up their malt forties against the stuccoed side of our house. Ha! we say. We laugh at your puny small-town dipsomaniacs.

"When's he getting here?"

"Five minutes ago."

There is no real estate agent coming, of course. We are waiting out in front of Sixpence House for Mr. Sharpe, the local contractor. From what we have heard of the Sixpence, we'll need to have a first look at the inside with a builder in constant attendance.

The Sixpence is a building with broad shoulders – big, lumbering, ancient, and crooked, and its sides are painted an odd shade of clay red; but you can scarcely see the paint for all the ivy upon it. You can tell that it is old because it is so sloppy and rounded looking. This is the most certain way of spotting a genuine old Tudor: they never quite manage to have any perfectly right angles. The house looks down upon us with the kind of little windows that they used back when glass was expensive. A curtain lifts up just slightly, then flutters back down. We hear a muffled giggle inside.

"Hmm."

"Not waiting long, I hope?" comes a voice behind us.

We turn back around.

"Mr. Sharpe?"

He nods and gives me a beefy handshake. He's a rugged fellow with a trimmed mustache and dust on his boots; I imagine he knew this place when it was a pub.

"Shall we go in?"

We knock on the door, and after a long pause, it slowly opens to reveal . . . nobody.

Then we look down.

"Hello," says a little boy in his underwear. "My name's Felix."

"Why, hello there, Felix! My name is *Jenny*. Is your mum in?"

"No." He does a little pirouette.

"Oh. Are there any grown-ups in?"

"Could be. That's a nice bag. How old's your baby?"

"Thank you. He's a year and a half. Could you see if there are any grown-ups in?"

He points again at Jennifer's plaid schoolbag. "Can I see your bag?"

"Yes. But will you see if someone's – "

He darts back into the house. *"Someone at the door!"* we hear him yell up the stairs.

He comes back out and examines the schoolbag. "I have a bag. Where'd you get your bag?"

"In London. On King's Road."

"I'm going to Australia. We're moving there."

"Really! Think you'll see kangaroos?"

"No."

"I bet you do."

"I bet I don't."

A woman emerges from inside and steers Felix away.

"Put a shirt on, Felix. Hello" – she ushers us in – "I'm the tenant's mother. I see you've met my grandson."

"Yes. He's a very nice boy."

"Mmm. I'll let you look about. Just let me know if you have any questions."

"Thanks."

We saunter around the enormous living room. This clearly used to be the pub, with its sturdy little hearth and a floor scratched by many a stool. It appears now to hold the remains of an art gallery.

Mr. Sharpe points upward. "You know, first thing I'd do is take that silly ceiling out."

"What's wrong with it?"

"You know there's another ceiling up there, don't you?"

We look at him blankly.

"Oh, yes," he continues. "The original floorboards and beams — the wood. That's how it looked when it was a pub. I remember it." He looks up and surveys it again, hands on his hips. "Oh, it'd be glorious."

You can tell that, in his mind, he is already taking a crowbar to the ceiling.

We wander around the house's interior; the old wooden floors roll and dip like waves beneath us. The whole dining room feels as if it is off plumb. The wallpaper in the stairwell is moldy and rotting, peeling off; in a child's room on the top floor, the wallpaper is obliterated by explosions of orange and green crayon. Nothing has been much maintained here.

The contractor is making measurements, poking at the walls.

"There's a basement, right?" I ask as I pick my way down the staircase.

"There certainly is," he says. "Old pubs always have a cellar for the kegs."

I open the door and peer down the stairs into darkness.

"Well?" Jennifer says.

"Maybe you and Morgan should stay up here."

"Okay." She doesn't sound too pained to hear this.

I find a light switch and, hunched over, clamber down the steps. The ceiling is scarcely five feet, and the floor is covered in loose, old planks and furniture, and swirling in an inch or two of water.

Mr. Sharpe looks in on me from the top of the stairs. "You'll be needing a sump there."

"Yes." I nod sagely. Whatever that is.

I look around in the semidarkness, hear the dripping water. I can see where they once rolled down the kegs from street level. I wonder how many laden kegs have rolled down those rails, and how many emptied ones have passed back up?

Drip, drip.

"Turn the switch," says a small voice.

"What?" I turn around. Mr. Sharpe is gone. Felix is standing there.

"The old switch by the stairs." He points. "Turn it on."

I look over by the stairs; there is indeed an old switch there, from the days of twine-insulated wiring.

"What's it for?"

"Turn it on," he says, strangely insistent.

And for a moment we just stand there, staring at each other in a weird impasse. He looks as if he is about to scream for his parents.

"Felix," I finally say, "I'm not turning that switch."

"Why not?" he demands.

"Because I'm not. It's not my house."

"But I live here."

"I'm not doing it."

"Turn the switch."

"No."

He waits a long moment, shrugs, and walks away. "Don't know why you won't," he mutters.

Back up in the living room, Jennifer and Sharpe are waiting for me.

"Well?"

"It's a cellar, all right."

"Your feet are wet," Jennifer says.

"I know."

"Back when it was pub," Sharpe recalls, "I used go down there to help roll up the barrels."

"Really?"

"That's right. And some days there'd be so much water down there that the barrels were *floating*."

We walk outside, and I can now see the big iron doors set into the ground for where the barrels went in. The door has a nasty crack running through its rusted plate face. That will need looking after; Jennifer already plunged through one such broken hatch some years ago while walking down a street in Inverness, gouging a bloody rut into her leg.

Cellar doors are never to be trusted, in any case. Yesterday I came across Walter Thornbury's 1865 book, *Haunted London*. The binding was totally shot, the sewing undone and the cover falling off, but I didn't care; it is wonderful book, not of ghost stories, but of a city's long-gone inhabitants, street by street and block by block. The guiding spirit of its haunting comes from its epigraph by Samuel Rogers:

> The West End seems to me one vast cemetery. Hardly a street but has in it a house once occupied by dear friends with whom I had daily intercourse: if I stopped and knocked now, who would know or take interest in me? *The streets to me are peopled with shadows: the city is as a city of the dead.*

There are many such haunted Londons, I think, and haunted New Yorks and Parises and San Franciscos as well.

It is while walking with the reader down one such fraught street in

St Giles that Thornbury recalls the very real ghouls that may lurk beneath the ground of this city of the dead:

A friend of mine remembers in his youth hurrying through Dyot-Street as through a dangerous defile. There was a legend at the time of a banker's clerk who, returning from his round, with his book of notes and bills fastened by the usual chain, as he passed down Dyot-Street, felt a cellar door sinking under him. Conscious of his danger, he made a spring forward, dashed down the street, and escaped the trap set for him by the thieves.

This is the stuff of nightmares. Can there be a more sickening sensation than the ground giving way underneath you, where grasping hands and slitting knives await? Jonathan Edwards was fond of saying that we are all walking on a rotten covering over the pit of hell, knowing not where our feet will plunge through; but bank clerks, it seems, have to walk over the really rotten parts.

Downstairs at Oscar's is crowded again today, but upstairs is wonderfully empty. I like it just fine this way. The tables and chairs are rustic, backlit by windows. There is a corner table, very wobbly, looking out over the street below. The table is nearly covered by a vase of sunflowers, and it has only one chair – a little child's chair. Clearly no one is meant to actually sit here; so, of course, I will. I grab a large chair, push the vase aside, and straddle the table's little legs with my knees to steady it while I pour my tea.

I am reading the papers. This is a daily ritual of mine: a hot drink, a table, and two (preferably three) of the day's papers. Britain is a marvelous place for this; they worship their papers here. Britons will scoff at this statement, but it is true. The morning TV news shows clip out articles from the latest papers, project them onto the TV screen, and spend part of the program *reading the newspaper to you*. The papers are an institution, and for good reason. In any American city, you are lucky to find one or two first-rate papers on the stands – maybe a copy of the *New York Times* or the *Wall Street Journal* – along with whatever thin gruel the local newspaper serves. But any British newsstand will have a heaped shelf of the *Guardian,* the *Independent,* the *Daily Telegraph,* and the *Times.*

The newspapers here now stand as a curious contrast to the magazines. In the mid-1960s, the *New York Times Book Review* would run full-page ads advertising a British Magazine-of-the-Month Club: one month you'd get *Encounter,* edited by Frank Kermode; another month, a copy of *Nova;* and then the inevitable *Blackwood's* would arrive. It wouldn't be much of a club now, as the magazine culture has become curiously anemic, save for perhaps *The Economist* and *Private Eye.* There is now a surfeit of aggressively moronic lad's mags, but no small-circulation zine culture, and no British equivalent of, say, *The New Yorker* or *Harper's* or the *Atlantic.*

But their newspapers are a complete joy. The headlines today are largely the same, of course: Blair dodging questions about the petrol strike, anti-Suharto demonstrators, the Olympics in Sydney, a debate between Hillary Clinton and Rick Lazio. I'll read the same news in several different papers, for it is like reading in stereo. Panned left, the piccolo twitterings of the *Independent;* panned right, the cello mutterings and groanings of the *Telegraph.*

And newspapers are *different* here: a glance at these front pages will immediately impress this fact upon you. First of all, the paper is always from London – even the Manchester *Guardian* is only a nominal exception, as their center of gravity is the London office. Britain has a tremendous concentration of media and culture in London. The recording, electronic, print, and broadcast media are all based there; as is, of course, the British government itself. The United

States are far more diffuse. Manhattan is the print capital, L.A. is the audiovisual capital, and Washington is the capital capital. And you ignore Chicago at your peril. But British journalism lives in the same few postal codes, works on the same few streets, drinks in the same few pubs. If you want to promote anything in Britain, you need never venture beyond the M25 ring road.

British papers do not hold up the fig leaf of objectivity, for they have no qualms about advocating causes; party affiliations are not limited to the editorial page. The *Independent* wants to legalize cannabis; the *Telegraph* wants to keep the Euro out; the *Guardian* wants genetically modified food off the shelves; and the *News of the World* wants pedophiles hog-tied and castrated. Indeed, when the *News* began an inept campaign of naming and shaming paroled sex offenders, their readership rioted enthusiastically, with vigilantes in one estate attacking the home of that most heinous sort of criminal, a *pediatrician*.

The papers even look different here. British stories have great structural integrity, because their newspapers do not employ jumps. A jump, in hack parlance, is where you only show part of a story on one page, then direct your readers to the hinterlands of page A20. American newspapers use such jumps so often that we think nothing of it. But it is not a benevolent layout decision. Editors know that with every jump, you lose a massive number of readers: few make it past the initial paragraphs. The *New York Herald* used this reader laziness to great effect on November 9, 1874, when its front page shouted:

A Shocking Sabbath Carnival of Death
Terrible Scenes of Mutilation

And if you were a *Herald* reader, you had a nasty shock: marauding carnival lions and elephants loosed upon the avenues had trampled and eaten forty-nine New Yorkers; why, Governor Dix himself was out in the street, stalking tigers with his shotgun! Citizens were too busy loading their guns and barring their doors to notice that, if you read further into the article, you were notified in small type that this story was a fiction to "test the city's preparedness to meet a catastrophe."

Details buried later in a story – the ones that tend to render it in rather grayer and more challenging terms than the monochrome summary initially tossed at you – are lost to most American readers. But not in Britain: the story is there for you in all its complex glory. Plus, they're easier to clip out.

And, the *Sun* has naked women on page 3. Like most of Europe, the British don't give much thought to bare breasts; well, the women don't, anyway. The effect on Americans is to make our own mores look peculiarly hysterical. But to understand this, first you have to buy the *Sun*.

I do not advise this.

Even the cartooning is different here. For all the well-thumbed British copies of *Viz, Beano,* and *Asterix,* the graphic novel cults of Clowes and Spiegelman never took hold in the UK. And yet, curiously, Britain has some of the world's finest editorial cartoonists. American editorial cartoons have an absolute craven desire to make sure that nobody, not even the ignoramuses who don't read the paper anyway, will miss their meaning. The American cartoonist labels every object in the frame. It is not enough to use a donkey and an elephant: you also have to helpfully label them DEMOCRATS and GOP, just in case someone hasn't had the idea explained to him yet. If you draw George W. Bush, you still have to write BUSH somewhere on his person. The American editorial cartoonist grabs you by the lapels and shakes you: "Do you get it? *Do you get it?* DO YOU GET THE JOKE?"

The British have a subtlety that puts stateside cartoonists to shame. There is, today, a cartoon in one paper depicting William Hague as the pope; he is being pinned down by a meteorite. First, the cartoonist is assuming that you will recognize an unlabeled William Hague, and that you will recognize the reference to his current agonies in the polls. And then – most astonishingly – that you will recognize a controversial installation piece by Maurizio Cattelan at the Royal Academy of Art, which shows a lifelike statue of the pope getting floored by meteorite that has crashed through a cathedral ceiling.

You cannot do this in America. There are only four works of art that American editorial cartoonists can refer to: the *Mona Lisa, Whistler's Mother, Washington Crossing the Delaware,* and *American Gothic*. If you work for a highbrow paper, you might get away with *Nighthawks*. Sculpture is limited to the Statue of Liberty, Mount Rushmore, and *The Thinker*. But that's it: nothing else from the last century is allowed, and certainly not anything from last week.

Moreover, this cartoon of William Hague is rendered in glorious color. It is an art here. We are in the land of Hogarth. Americans can put color in weather maps and useless pie charts, but not newspaper cartoons. Those only get colored ink for their Sunday installments of *Family Circus* and *Cathy*.

I leaf onward past the *Guardian* cartoon, and I am stopped cold by a headline:

Fancy a Seat in the Lords? Apply Now

What? A lord? That's the job for me!

For my stateside readers who are unfamiliar with this noble institution, allow me to explain: the House of Lords originated in a hereditary system, which is a sort of governance by copulation. A spermocracy, if you will. This gene pool has since expanded into a truly unsettling combination of bucktoothed familial toffs and gin-soaked party-patronage appointees. But the prime minister, it appears, has now decided that there shall be seven or eight "people's peers" in the House of Lords. And the criteria are stringent indeed: "Lord Stephenson denied there were any plans for Big Brother–style evictions of people's peers who failed to contribute effectively to the Lords, saying: 'We won't be appointing any duds.' "

Say . . . I am a good British citizen. I am no *dud*. And I do fancy a seat in the Lords. I rush home – Morgan latches onto my left leg for the last ten yards across the apartment – and I pick up the phone.

"British Civil Service."

"Hello . . ." I suddenly worry, absurdly, that my big American accent will disqualify me from the Lords. What if she is taking notes?

"Yes?" she presses.

So I ask meekly, in an irritatingly anglicized voice, which, like that of Paul Theroux, indicates that I may be a distant relative of Thurston Howell III:

"Hello, I'd like to be a lord."

"You mean a people's peer?"

"Yes. That's what they're calling them?"

There is a small but agonizing pause. "All right, then," she sighs. "I will send you an application."

Chapter Fifteen
Beholds THE LORD

Oʜ, ʙᴏʏ! I'm going to be a lord!

The first thing to do, I decide, is learn all about lords. In most of the world, the Lord is an older gentleman with unkempt hair and flowing robes, seen in the vicinity of cloud banks with lots of vertical shafts of sunlight. He has a predilection for wiping out cattle. He is inordinately fond of praise.

British lords share the latter characteristic, but the similarities end there. I am stymied at finding any evidence of these lords on television. What do the lords do, exactly? There is, unfortunately, no C-SPAN in this country. What they do have, instead, is a sliver of coverage from the House of Commons. The weekly Question Time there is a strangely riveting spectacle. MPs of the governing party ask their prime minister fawning questions on party-approved topics – such as whether water is wet, whether snow is cold, and whether ice cream is delicious. The opposing party, in turn, challenges these claims, asserting that water is in fact quite dry this year, that the snow is distinctly warmer, and that ice cream is noticeably less wholesome and creamy than it was under the previous government.

This noble travesty drags on for half an hour every week, during which all statements must be in the form of a question. MPs are generous in their interpretation of what a question is. Their inquiries take three basic forms. There is the inquiry into the other party's moral putrefaction: "Madame Speaker, is my colleague too busy with his rent boys and autoerotic experimentation to see to the proper distribution of health care in his district?"; there is the statement of derogation, followed by a request for verification: "Madame Speaker, the prime minister and his minions have allowed our government to once again fall into the same absurd policies that did not work the last time they were in power. Isn't that true?"; and there is the coup de grâce, which may only be used by the leader of one party against his opposite: "I don't see the point in answering these questions when the questioner is likely to be voted out by his own party in the very near future. Am I not correct?"

Once the appropriate form of questioning has been engaged, the MPs must then engage in guttural sounds of approval or dismay. They cannot clap or cheer or utter recognizable words – unless *Rew-wah! Rew-wah! Rew-wah!* and *Hyaw! Hyaw! Hyaw!* are words that I've somehow managed to miss from my dictionary.

I love it. I watch it every week.

We run into the Ratcliffes outside Seven Stars Inn.

"Jennifer!" Mrs. Ratcliffe says. "Have you found a house yet?"

"I think so. Sixpence House."

We turn to Mr. Ratcliffe, the authority on all local matters. "What do you know about the Sixpence?"

"A bit."

"You've been in there?"

"I lived there," he says dryly. "From 1954 to 1970."

"No!"

"Yes. Till it stopped being a pub. I lived upstairs."

"And?"

161

"When I put my shirts in the closet at night, they came out wet in the morning."

Then Mrs. Ratcliffe remembers something: her daughter, who is on the fire brigade, had to help pump out the house's cellar last spring.

"Place has been on the market for ages. It's gone through a few owners."

It is, in other words, a millstone.

We decide to take it.

Here's the funny thing about buying real estate in Britain: if a survey has been done on the property, they don't have to show it to you. You have to go and get your own, which means that a house for sale can get surveyed three or four times in a month. Britain, I gather, is a fine place to be a building surveyor.

"We really want to make an offer," I tell Martin Like. "How long will it take you to do an engineering survey on Sixpence?"

"I, I, I have to contract it out to a fellow, and he's quite busy." Martin's hands make paper-shuffling motions. "It could be a number of days. At least a week. Or more. I'm . . . I'm not quite sure."

I have nothing much to do at Booth's now, either. So Jennifer and I decide to make a family field trip of a few days into Hereford, which is the nearest place with a rail station, a cathedral, and chain stores. We're to stay at some place called Hedley Lodge, which I don't know anything about other than that it has queen-size beds.

Our bus to Hereford is going to leave in about twenty minutes. I haul our bags down and wait for Jennifer and Morgan in the courtyard. The door, I notice, is open into Mr. Wiggington's workshop.

Brian Wiggington is a downstairs tenant who runs a furniture restoration workshop out in our building's courtyard. I often see him as I walk out, deep in concentration as he refinishes some long-neglected table or cabinet found in a local farmhouse. He has beautiful eighteenth-century chairs and tables by his workbench, but that is not what I have been eyeing lately. Hanging outside the shop is an ancient saw, at least a century in age by the look of it. I pass by it every day on my way out of the house, and I have a morbid fascination with it. The saw is dangling from a wooden peg, and over it is a slate with chalked-in numbers. The slate has been something of a work in progress over the last few weeks:

```
        Old Saw for Sale
              £10
              £9
              £8
              £7
              £6
              £5
              £4
              £3
              £2
              £1
             Free
```

Brian sees me staring at the sign as he steps out of his shop.

"Want a saw?"

"Not just yet. I'm waiting for the price to drop further."

He lights his pipe at this.

"How's the househunting?" he asks, puffing.

"Nothing yet. But we've got our eye on Sixpence House."

"Really now?"

"We need to look at its structure more closely."

"You have to, place that old."

"Yeah. Though a survey costs six hundred pounds alone. If there's tens of thousands of pounds in repairs needed, I don't know if we'll be able to offer the asking price."

"What're they asking?"

"One twenty-five. They claim that another couple wants to make an offer on it too."

Brian regards his pipe thoughtfully. "I'd be careful with prices. People in Hay" – puff – "have been becoming a little greedy of late. A great deal of new money flowing in here, you know. Wasn't always like this." Puff. "Don't know if it can last."

"Hmm."

Brian looks up through the cloud of smoke at the sky above. "Looks to be nice weather today."

That's a comfort, I suppose, though riding the local bus can be terrifying even in good weather. To an American, the country lanes here are ludicrously narrow, really just a single lane. The last time I went into Hereford, our bus bounced merrily down the little road and obliterated everything in its path: hedges, jackdaws, and the occasional Morris Minor. At one point the driver slammed on the brakes suddenly, throwing us all forward; women screamed, and I smashed my knee against the seat in front of me. We'd nearly hit a massive electric-company cherry picker parked squarely in the middle of the road. The bus inched ahead past it, and I rubbed the swelling goose egg on my patella.

A friend of mine once took a bus deep into the Amazon; every time they approached the crest of a hill, he'd see the driver pray and rub a crucifix mounted to the dash. When I've ridden the local bus from Hay, rather than being surrounded by women clutching chickens and small children, I usually wind up next to a couple of ruddy-faced middle-agers reading the soccer supplement in the tabloids. But the overall effect is much the same.

Jennifer emerges into the courtyard with Morgan. "We don't need to take the bus! Julian Blunt says he'll drive us."

"That," I tell her, "is very good news indeed."

I hear about Julian all the time; we are living in his and Diana's building, after all. But I have never met him before. He is a trim man with hair going white, and quiet – not quite the forceful personality that Diana is. It is easy to see how the two complement each other's angles.

The hedgerows are rushing by, and Morgan is hypnotized by the blur of green.

"So," asks Jennifer, "you work in antiques?"

"Yes." Julian glances from the road. "The space that Pemberton's is in now, that used to be my shop."

"When was that?"

"Oh" – he brushes back a lock of hair – "I first arrived in – I don't know, 1973? Though my mother had family all around this area. A friend of mine from university and I worked together. Back in those days was before the Welsh countryside had been picked over. Those were amazing days."

He smiles with the recollection as we pass over the pretty little bridge by the Bredwardine vicarage.

"Every day," he continues, "you could wake up and know for a fact that in the course of a week you'd find something unbelievable in a barn or a farmhouse or an estate somewhere. The whole area was wide-open for us. Over time, of course, it got harder – until eventually, it was like anywhere else, where you only get a fantastic find if you're really lucky. People around here are more aware of what things are worth now."

"*Antiques Roadshow* must be the bane of your existence now."

"No, not at all. I think it's wonderful. Really. The things people bring in to that show! The most amazing things, items that they've been taking care of even when they *don't know what it is*." He shakes his head in disbelief. "They just know it's old. It's quite heartening, really – you see how there are mountains of paintings and furniture out there still being preserved by the public."

I look out the window and over the fields and apple orchards at the sagging Tudor homes wreathed by trees in the distance.

"Are you still doing antiques?"

"At this moment I'm creating bookshelves for a client."

"Must be a roaring trade in those around here."

"Yes, particularly for this client. He's got a barn up in the Black Hills, and a place in London too. An expert in Eastern European politics, does a lot of advising for the government, that sort of thing. Anyway, his father, a very learned man living in New York, died about six months ago. And so when his son went back to go through the estate, he had to go through the old man's library. His father had been a keen collector of books, especially of early American litera-ture. But I don't know if anyone knew just how much he had. It filled four cargo containers. They shipped it all over to London; part of it will be getting auctioned off next year. And the rest" – he gestures to the hills – "will be up there."

Hidden up in these hills. Perhaps they will be discovered again by another Julian Blunt, or another Richard Booth, in another fifty years.

The car stops suddenly.

A fire truck is blocking one lane, and in the other the traffic is being waved along a few cars at a time. When it comes our turn, we drive through cautiously, and from behind the fire truck we see a completely gutted BMW. The windshield is blown out, and the frame all twisted. Police are milling about.

"Mmm," muses Julian. "Never know what you'll find up in the hills."

Hedley Lodge, it turns out, is run by Benedictine monks of the Belmont Abbey. So if you steal the towels, you're going to hell. We don't realize any of this until the man behind the front desk stands up to help us, and he's wearing a black robe.

This place has big rooms, with equally big, lurid crucifixes over their doors.

"I think" – Jennifer flops down onto the bed with a notebook – "that I am going to work on my book."

"I'll take Morgan out back. Give you some peace and quiet."

My boy and I venture outside and around the side of the hotel. It is not your typical hotel chain: here there is a cemetery filled with departed Brothers of the monastery. The graves are mossy, old, though toward the front of the cemetery are a few new ones. You can tell which ones are new because there's still a rounded mound of dirt over the grave, from where the coffin has displaced the earth. Walk back, though, past the ones buried about fifty years ago or so, and you start seeing people-sized depressions in front of each headstone. It's shocking to see, really, these collapsed graves, to look at one and know that here the coffin has rotted away, and the earth presses down upon the monk's ears and teeth and fingers – that right here, under your feet, is a man, or what once was a man, in the final stages of decomposition into dirt himself. You just don't see that in the modern U.S. cemetery, where the ground is kept flat and green as a billiard table. There is no hint that, heaven forbid, a body is buried underneath.

We walk past these and out back, to hedges and arches and rosebushes and a wide, graveled path. In one soaring hedge arch I look up and see, suspended and thickly hidden in the woody growths, a rusted old schoolroom chair.

Two men in black suits come crunching up the gravel walk and pass us.

"Hello," one of them says cheerfully.

"Hello."

They walk on to a remote corner of the grounds, disappearing behind a distant hedge.

The evening is beginning to fall now. Morgan and I trot around the paths, and he stops to pick handfuls of little stones and toss them about. And as we turn a corner around a hedge into a secluded corner, there it is:

An open grave.

It is empty, waiting: just a blank headstone, a pile a of dirt with a tarp over it, and corrugated tin weighted by some rocks to cover the gaping pit, which peeks out from beneath. Morgan charges at it, and I snatch him up.

The men in black, it dawns on me, were undertakers. As we leave the gardens, I see their rather sporty-looking hearse pulled up to the rear of the hotel, to the monks' quarters. It is disgorging a coffin out the back. I look instinctively at my watch, then think, for that fellow over there, in his wooden box, time has stopped.

It is not a new conceit, I suppose. A charming writer of trivia and miscellany in the nineteenth century, John Timbs, came up with one of the best book titles ever, *Things Not Generally Known,* and in his 1867 book, *Wonderful Inventions,* he has a bizarre passage on the long-intertwined history of watches and death:

In early times, watches were often made in the forms of skulls and coffins, suggested, doubtless, by the solemnity of the flight of time. Sir John Dick Lauder has a Death's-head watch, which belonged formerly to Mary, Queen of Scots . . . The forehead of the skull bears the symbols of death, the scythe and the hourglass, placed between a palace and a cottage, to show the impartiality of the grim destroyer; at the back of the skull is Time destroying all things, and at the top of the head are scenes of the Garden of Eden and the Crucifixion. The watch is opened by reversing the skull, placing the upper part of it in the hollow of the hand, and lifting the jaw by a hinge . . . The works of the watch form the brains of the skull, and are within a silver envelope, which acts as a musically-toned bell; while the dial-plate is in the place of the palate.

Just in case Mary's windup skull ever got a concussion that knocked its ticking brains out of whack, she also had a second watch that she could always rely on. This one was in the shape of a coffin.

I could tell you about all the usual tourist stuff in Hereford: the big cathedral, the medieval chained library, and the town's ancient and still thriving cider industry. But what I really notice about the town is this: there is a disturbing abundance of street signs in Hereford pointing you to the local crematorium. When you get lost in Hereford, you might not know where to go – but you'll always know *where you're going to go.*

In a land inhabited as long and as densely as this one, there's not much room for sentimentality about these things. The ground here is chockablock with dead folk. Dead people hold such a solid majority in Britain that if they could run and vote in elections, they'd win every time. So the crematorium, I suppose, is much needed, as there has been debate here of late about how to dispose of the abundance of useless encoffined citizenry. Britain's graveyards have become so packed, elbow to bony elbow, that Parliament is now reconsidering rolling back an old prohibition against upright burial and the reuse of grave sites. Really, can any dead person be said to be *using* their grave in the first place?

It has long been impossible to develop any part of this country without digging up somebody, though people are more respectful now than they used to be. I once came across a letter to the editor of *Notes and Queries* magazine, from about a century ago, complaining that after a churchyard was "moved" to make way for new houses, the writer walked down a street to discover that the tombstones of his parents had been reused as paving stones. In the December 1, 1883, issue of that same magazine, another writer recalled a London friend watching the Holborn Viaduct being cut through the burial ground of St. Andrew's church:

> He was looking down at the works from a lofty window near, and watching especially a certain labourer, who was busily shovelling out the unconsidered coffins and skeletons of eighteenth century Londoners. This man amused himself by arranging the skulls of his victims all a-row among the edge of the hole in which he was working. But presently the sight of so many ghastly human heads, staring at him with their empty eyeholes, seemed to affect even his imagination, and my friend saw him stop in his work and deliberately turn all the skulls around, *so that they should not look at him.*

It takes a lot of skulls to spook a Brit. Their practicality in such matters is rooted, perhaps, in that there are few churches here to promulgate the Great Fearsome Mystery of the Hereafter.

Even though religion is little observed here, the Sunday TV is full of it – thanks to a state religion, there is a far greater religious presence on television here than on U.S. broadcast networks. It is a curious inversion of America, where you can't show naked breasts or have people taking the Lord's name in vain, but where you will also never have church services on any major network. But perhaps

British religion has been domesticated and tamed through a long comic tradition of mock sermons; the novelist Kyril Bonfiglioli used to amuse himself during his retirement on the isle of Jersey by writing reviews of *church services* for a local magazine under the invented persona of one "Karl Bellamy." You can still open newspapers to headlines like the one in the *Guardian* today: BIBLE'S KING DAVID EXPOSED AS A DESPOT WHO DID NOT KILL GOLIATH.

This country has not always been so casual in its theology. Several hundred years ago, Lord Berkeley lamented, "An argument between divines proceeds like this. It is so. It is not so. It is so. It is not so. It is so." Britain was one of the most argumentative countries in the world, a placed so riven by religion that, after the dissident William Tracy had the temerity to die of natural causes, rather than going to the gallows like any decent blasphemer, enraged opponents dug him up just so they could torture his rotten corpse and burn it at the stake.

Of course, they'd dig him up and burn him today too. They need the grave space.

There has been, for some time now, a billboard visible from the Amtrak line as it enters New Jersey. It reads:

> Jesus Christ: The Lord of Newark

To which the only appropriate response, really, is: "Yeah, well, he can *have* it."

But he cannot, I think, have Britain any more. It is not so much that the forces of atheism have triumphed in the land of Darwin, it is just that theologians have withered away into public irrelevance. Great Britain has one of the lowest rates of church attendance in the world, and every year more churches are shut down. The monks working here at our hotel have become the exception rather than the rule. You cannot find a town here that hasn't either a ruined church, an abandoned priory, or a vicarage long gone to seed or converted into a condo, a bed-and-breakfast, or an art gallery. Such conversions are so common that they hardly elicit notice.

When the gory Victorian novelist George Lippard wanted a setting for his archdemon Gold-Bug to unleash Armageddon on the city of Philadelphia, it was from a headquarters in a rotting church. In the United States, there is an illicit and unholy thrill in taking over a desanctified church, even now; a major Manhattan venue for chemically refreshed dancing through the nineties was an old Sixth Avenue church. There is something more shocking in the death of a religious space in America, more haunting. Britain, by all rights, should be the more haunted place; religion is ancient here, and old Christian churches squat on the sites of even older chapels, which were themselves built over druid ruins and the like. And yet, when you see an aged and crumbled chapel here – the roof caved in, the windows empty, the graves long overgrown and the memorial slabs worn away by the wind and water – you are moved by the aesthetic sublimity of it all. Wordsworth might have been made wistful and mournful by many things at Tintern Abbey, but the death of a religious order wasn't one of them.

But a religious space in the United States, once abandoned, has the acrid whiff of blasted hope, the pathos of ardent belief destroyed. I know of no spookier place in San Francisco than the empty lot in the Fillmore where the People's Temple once stood, before Jim Jones took his congregation on their fatal exodus to Guyana. Even the most pathetic monuments retain this sort of power. I went up to Hartford with a girlfriend one Thanksgiving to meet her parents, and as we drove down I-84 past Waterbury, I noticed a tall, lit cross on a distant hilltop.

"What's up there?"

"Oh, that's just Holy Land."

"What?"

"Holy Land U.S.A.? It's a religious amusement park — why are you laughing? — I'm serious. You haven't heard of it?"

"No. I have to see this."

"It went out of business."

"Oh."

And so it had. I found out later that some nuns owned it now, and a pious local businessman still paid the electric bill to keep its giant neon cross lit, but otherwise, there was nothing up in those hills but a ghostly midway and ruined exhibits on popes and miracles. It became a favored spot for local teens to get stoned, drink wine coolers, and spin doughnuts with their cars. Stand up there on a winter day, with the wind moaning through the broken bottles and whipping the power lines, and you behold the barest ruined choir of all — something more sorrowful than even the loneliest little ruined chapel in all the moors of Scotland.

Chapter Sixteen
Can't Think of a
Good Title

I AM STAGGERING up the third flight of stairs with my luggage and with Morgan slung over my shoulder like a twenty-pound sack of biter biscuits when Diana sees me.

"You're going for House of Lords?" she blurts out.

"What? Oh . . . uh . . ."

And now she becomes flustered too. "Your mail's up there. I opened it by accident. Plain brown envelope and all." Of course it's a plain brown wrapper, the House of Lords must be discreet with its products by mail. "Then I saw House of Lords and thought, good heavens. And then I looked at the envelope and saw it was your name on it." And then she folds her hands helplessly.

"Of course."

I suppose it is difficult for Diana to avoid seeing my mail. It all passes through her hands for the simple reason that there are no mailboxes here. American suburbanites will find this puzzling, but just as in many cities in America, British mail always comes through a slot in your front door. This is true in cities and countryside alike; the sides of their streets are not dotted with tin boxes atop wooden posts.

In the 1930s, the puppeteer Walter Wilkinson wrote a series of popular reminiscences on his travels with a Punch and Judy show across the British countryside. Inevitably, the call came for him to try an

America tour. In the resulting 1938 book, *Puppets Through America,* he actually has to *explain* the concept of mailboxes to his British readers:

> The mail-box is a curious construction that all country Americans put out on the road so that the postman can drive up, take the letters out for despatch, and leave for any delivery. It is a long, narrow, metal box with a curved top supported on a post some four or five feet high. Every house has one – they go on, all along the roads, three thousand miles across the continent . . . Some posts wriggle and some are straight; they lean at different angles, they are different heights, and different ages, in fact, it could be said that the mail-box is the one thing through which country Americans express their individuality.

Wilkinson also marvels at a number of other mysteries of American innovation to his readers, including central heating, iced drinks, commercial radio, room service, roadside diners, and ventilation-grate louver handles that are actually labeled OPEN and SHUT. This last detail in particular amazes Wilkinson. British manufacturers, you understand, have a great aversion to labeling the buttons and levers on their household devices, lest it be discovered that they never worked in the first place.

But it is indeed true that in America you can go months without seeing anything more of your postman than a bronzed arm reaching out of a white Jeep, stuffing a ration of advertising circulars into your box. Here people have a rather more personal relation with postal carriers; they come up to your house on foot. You see them; they see you. If the BBC children's show *Postman Pat* is to be believed, the result is that letter carriers spend their entire day drinking tea and petting cats in the living rooms of old ladies. In the deepest rural areas, hitching rides with the local postman is not altogether unknown; his may be the only public vehicle for the area. In America, trying to climb into any mailman's car will get you zapped with a Taser.

But woe and alas to those who block the righteous path of Her Majesty's letter carriers. Witness this report in the February 24, 1844, issue of the *Illustrated London News,* in which a postman, his way to the mail slot having been blocked by the plaintiff, had apparently delivered "a violent blow in the face" to the fellow:

CLERKENWELL. – On Thursday James Tredgear, a letter carrier, was charged by Waddington, the gaoler of this court, with having assaulted him in the execution of his duty, and also with having conducted himself disorderly in the passage leading to the court. When the defendant was placed at the bar before the magistrate, he had his hat on, and persisted in wearing it, although the usher had previously desired him to uncover. – The Clerk: *Why don't you take your hat off, sir, in the presence of the magistrate?* – Defendant: *What's that to you? What am I to take my hat off for?* – Clerk: *Out of respect for the court, sir.* – Defendant: *I'm in her Majesty's service as well as that gentleman there* (pointing at the magistrate), *and you see he sits with his hat on.* – The dispute on this point of etiquette was terminated by the usher quietly knocking off the defendant's hat, and taking it from him. – The Clerk: *What is your name?* – Defendant: *What's it to you? I might as well ask you what your name is!*

The final result of this mighty showdown between the judicial and the postal branches of government is not known.

When I get upstairs, I open the envelope. I know that it is a British letter without even looking at it, for British mail looks and feels different from American mail. It is strangely old-fashioned. British envelopes are often made of unbleached paper, brown and coarse, and not entirely unlike the paper towels in a lavatory. This paper is also used on their parcels, for I have never received a package in just a box; it is always carefully wrapped in brown parcel paper. And the stamps! Row after row of pictures of Her Majesty; like old alabaster locket engravings. The different denominations do not get different pictures, only different colors of ink: here is the queen in blue, the queen in mauve, the queen in green. Collecting British stamps would be a short-lived hobby.

The application to become a peer looks like the world's most boring grant application. The requirements are rather simple. You must be over twenty-one, surely a crushing disappointment to the youth of Britain. And you must be British, which is also unfortunate, as it might have been a splendid jobs scheme for refugees. This is because there are no government plans or programs in Great Britain, only schemes. To Americans – for whom scheming is what con men engage in – there is something delightful in this British turn of phrase, in watching news conferences where government ministers answer reporters by stating flatly, "Yes. I have a *scheme* to deal with that problem."

Scheming sounds about right: for the application says you can also be a convicted criminal. "The Commission," it drones, "will take into account convictions for serious criminal offences but believes strongly in the rehabilitation of offenders."

I'm sure Lord Archer will be pleased to hear that.

One of the sections is titled "Modernizing the House of Lords." This is a curious notion, for either you accept the premise of hereditary government or you do not. If you do accept its premise, you cannot modernize the Lords by letting in The People; and if you do not accept its premise, then the only logical modernization for the

House of Lords is to clear out the hereditary lords. Saying that you will modernize something does not make it so, or even make it humanly possible. Back in California, I used to buy plastic bags of ice that bore this motto:

> *Ice*
> *As Modern as Tomorrow*

I pointed this out to my roommate Mike, a man who now VPs for a large ad agency.

"Hmm," he explained.

Remember, this product was *frozen water*.

Modernize the House of Lords? You might as well try to modernize the stones under your shoes. They too, I am sure, are *as modern as tomorrow*. So I toss the application aside, half filled in; I haven't even thought of who my references will be. I don't suppose I can be a lord after all. In any case, I lack breeding – not to mention inbreeding.

All the titles for my book have been shot down.

Walking on the Rings of Saturn?

"Sounds too much like another book called *The Rings of Saturn*," my editor says. But he has a suggestion:

Profiles in Discourage.

"Commercial suicide," Dave e-mails.

All right. Back to the drawing board with a cup of tea and some digestive biscuits. I emerge from my room several hours and many cross-outs later and beam with pride at Jennifer.

The Man with N-Ray Eyes.

"Too flippant," she says.

It is irritating, because I had a good title already. My book was originally called *Loser: A Brief History of Notable Failures*. But American publishers don't like this. Losing is a bad thing in our country. It's not allowed.

"Honestly," one editor said to me, "I don't think most Americans want to be seen walking around with a book that says LOSER on it in big letters."

Curiously, European publishers like the title. You may infer whatever you like about Europeans from this. I'm just happy not to have to rename it for them, for coming up with a title is not an easy task. Some authors, such as W. Somerset Maugham, gave up on titling altogether. His novel *The Moon and Sixpence* is so named because he thought it a pretty phrase; it has nothing to do with the book. But you can also be too descriptive. There is an 1829 broadsheet titled "To the Curious: The Word Scissars Appears Capable of More Variations in Spelling Than Any Other," with 480 spellings listed. After reading that title, you probably will not read on to discover that the variants of *scissors* include *sisszyrs* and *cyzsyrs*.

Nor, I suspect, will you be lured into Mary Godolphin's 1867 tome, *Robinson Crusoe, in Words of One Syllable* – she has to fudge a little and leaves in the name Friday – and I do not see much of a future for the peculiarly misbegotten 1937 project by J. Barlow Brooks, *Th' Amazin' Stories o' th' Bible: I' th' Lankisher Dialect*. If you would like to imagine God Almighty addressing Archangel Raphael in the persona of a farmer up to his wellies in pig slop, Mr. Barlow is happy to oblige: "If Aw wer thee, Rafe, Aw'd stop wittherin'! What yo' Ark-angils need to larn's a bit o' patience."

Any title is a balancing act. Your title cannot be too obscure, for nobody will remember what they are looking for when they go to the store. But it cannot be too familiar, because someone else will most certainly have used it. The later along you are in literary history, the more likely it is that someone has already used the title that you are thinking of. Every part of every nursery rhyme is now accounted for: there is a book called *Row Row Row Your Boat,* another called *Gently Down the Stream,* one called *Merrily Merrily Merrily,* and several laying claim to *Life Is But a Dream.* F. Scott Fitzgerald and his ilk strip-mined Shakespeare so thoroughly that only a few indefinite articles and conjunctions are left, and the Bible was gutted long ago, especially Proverbs and Ecclesiastes. Do not even think about using anything from the Song of Solomon. Nor, for that matter, can you use *Song of Solomon* itself as a title.

Do not be clever in trying to circumvent these restrictions; you will fail. People looking for Ruth Reichl's *Comfort Me with Apples* may instead be led astray to Peter de Vries's long-neglected 1956 novel of the same name, whose protagonist Chick Swallow spent a childhood in which he "was read to sleep with the classics and spanked with obscure quarterlies" – for there were already at least four books using the Solomonic *Comfort Me with Apples* when Reichl shoveled yet another onto the pile.

In fact, all fruits, gems, and celestial objects are also accounted for.

Southern novelists – the ones who use quirky names and look-at-me-I'm-so-eccentric characters – have vacuumed up all possible titles using familial relations, gospel hymns, and assorted poor-folk delicacies; so you can no longer use, say, *Mama,* or *Mama's Cornbread,* or *God Made the Earth, and Mama Made the Cornbread.* An unkind man might hope that, every permutation thus having been exhausted, this genre of literature will instantly drop dead. But I am not an unkind man.

A proper name is a better bet, though even here there is keen competition. I once considered naming a novel *Digby,* which struck me as a suitably Dickensian moniker, until I discovered that several other authors had already had precisely the same brilliant thought.

But the book was never published anyway, and this saved me the trouble of finding a better title.

The current world champion at titling – the man who holds the Title Title – would have to be Tibor Fischer, with *Don't Read This Book If You're Stupid* and *I Like Being Killed*. I do not know Fischer, but I like to imagine that he is an irritable man, prone to throwing books at people during readings and roaring: *You should be grateful to have my book denting your empty heads!*

Some books have their only moment of glory in their title page: everything past there is downhill. Jennifer and I have a weakness for such books. In our living room is a permanently wedded pair of faded Victorian children's books, respectively titled *Miss Nonentity* and *Blown to Bits*. The existence of the one simply dictated the acquisition of the other, even though both are perfectly dreadful pieces of writing. Next to them is a whole string of detective fiction from one publishing house in London back in the 1940s, bearing names like *You'll End Up Dead* and *I'll Say She Does*. My personal favorite would have to be a memoir, though: *Confessions of an Author's Wife,* published anonymously by Margaret Stringer in 1927. If you are a writer, this is a fine title to leave out on the coffee table. Unfortunately, Stringer never manages to top her title page, though her book's dedication comes close:

To
My Darling Husband
Without Whose Help These Confessions
Might Easily Have Been Finished Six Months Ago.

And without everyone else involved in my book, I'd have had a title six months ago. My editor continues to lob suggestions at me by e-mail and on the phone.

"What about *Banvard's Folly?*" he suggests at one point.

"Don't be silly," I mutter under my breath.

"Is the Sixpence survey in yet?" I press Martin.

"N-no, not yet. They've done the survey. But the report is still being prepared."

I saunter back out into the Bull Ring. A swirling damp has settled upon the town, and I wander the streets awhile for no good reason other than that it makes me happy; and I accomplish nothing other than occasionally jotting notes to myself in a little notepad, the writer's incorrigible habit. In a place like Hay, I am usually just scribbling down titles of interesting books, but occasionally my sojourns in the bookstores will generate existential jottings like *Alistair MacLean in a leatherbound set – WHY?*

I trudge down the road leading out of town, past an old farmhouse with what appears to be arrow slits in its side – this was indeed a border town – and make my way over to the supermarket. It is cool and coolly lit inside; I linger by a service counter selling film and batteries and notice an entry in the Customer Comments book that lies open upon it:

> *Why don't you have BRITISH apples? The ones you carry are French. This is an agricultural area with many orchards and surely you can stock our apples.*

It is a dirty culinary secret in this country that many English apples are distinctly inferior, really only suitable for making cider or baking. When one prominent chef scoffed at native Bramleys, preferring to use Granny Smiths from France, he was roundly cursed out by the farmers. But British soil does have its uses: the carrots here are so much more flavorful than American ones that they hardly seem to belong to the same botanical family.

An aproned teen is in the Co-op store, stocking a refrigerated case, and in the next aisle a young girl is tugging on her mother's hand and asking, how do they make biscuits?

"Shut it," the mother snaps.

My heart sinks; as it has repeatedly just this week. First on Wye Bridge, a young mother steering her girl out of my way, spitting "clumsy" at her; then a father bodily carrying a kicking little boy of perhaps three down the street, the boy howling, and the father saying through gritted teeth, "You shall not run away from me"; and then in McDonald's in Hereford, a father warning his four- or five-year-old, "Don't you dare move," from his spot on the bench, in a tone that spoke of many beatings away from the public eye. Twice I saw parents with children on a leash, in one case a child that was at least five years old. That one was running up toward me, quite a beautiful child, before being jerked back by his father. A very useful device, I'm sure, for reining the little ones in. And yet disturbing nonetheless. I, apparently, wore one of these leashes as a child; and my parents brought me up thus under the confused stares of our American neighbors.

When I get back to The Apartment, it is strangely quiet.

"We need to call the doctor," Jennifer yells down to me.

"What?" I pound up the stairs.

Jennifer is nursing Morgan, and he is whimpering.

"The big cast-iron doorstop – he pulled it over onto his foot."

I shrink back. The thing is a brutal old piece of metal, and it must weigh twenty pounds. My son does not know his own strength yet; nor did we. His tiny toes are swollen and crusted with blood.

"I'll get Diana."

I charge down into Pemberton's.

"Where's the nearest doctor?" I blurt.

"What's happened?"

"Morgan's foot is banged up. It's swollen."

"Is it broken?"

"I don't know. I don't think so. Maybe."

"Have you tried callendbluhbluh and arniwhawha."

"What?"

"Have you tried callendbluhbluh and arniwhawha."

"Pardon?"

Diana sighs and writes the words down on the back of a packing slip: *arnica pills, calendula ointment.*

"What are they?"

"They'll have them over at the chemist's. It's what I use for my daughter. The arnica is homeopathic."

For my readers outside of California and Vermont, or who do not subscribe to the *Utne Reader,* allow me to explain: *homeopathic* means that its active ingredient is absolutely not a goddamned thing.

"Are there any doctors around here?" I press. "The kind with cold stethoscopes and metal furniture?"

"There's the clinic. I can drive you there."

"Thanks!" I bolt back upstairs.

Diana leaves Hazel in charge of the store, and we buckle Morgan into his car seat.

"The clinic's just over on Forest Road," Diana says as we start off. "It's not far at all."

Jennifer and I are nervously fussing over Morgan, peering at his foot. He seems to have forgotten about the injury entirely; we are just bugging him now.

"So," Diana tries to distract us, "how's working for Booth?"

"Oh, it's been fine. But I finished a couple weeks ago. I don't know if he'll want me to do more. He might."

"So, not tempted to join the book trade?"

"I don't know. I'm already in it, I guess, just on the other end."

"What about you?" Jennifer asks Diana. "How long have you had Pemberton's?"

"Me?" Diana is taken a little aback. "Oh, that's not the only shop I've had. I've moved three times already."

"All in Hay?"

"Well, I started in a little arts and crafts shop, a stall really, in Hereford. Some friends convinced me to carry books too. That was about 1980. And it just blossomed from there . . . eventually I moved into the current store." She pulls into a parking space. "Pemberton's had been an antique shop covering several floors. Julian, you know. And then I moved into there and here I am. And here you are," she points at the clinic.

The doctor says Morgan's foot will be fine; we just have to keep the cut clean.

The receptionist, though, looks altogether more grave.

"The visit's normally covered under national health," she says apologetically, "but since you aren't residents . . ."

"Yes?"

We once made an emergency visit to a doctor in Oregon to get a large splinter out of Morgan's foot, and the clinic tried to bill us five hundred dollars. And that time was without any blood or swelling.

Jennifer and I brace ourselves.

". . . it will be twenty pounds."

We gape. "What?"

"I'm sorry!" the receptionist pleads. "It's terrible, isn't it?"

"You . . . think . . ."

"Is it different in your country?"

We stare uncomprehendingly at her.

"Yes," I finally say. "It is different in our country."

Chapter Seventeen
Is at Death's Doorknob

WE ARE MAKING plans: brilliant, brilliant plans.

"Here's the first floor," says Jennifer, spreading out graph-paper diagrams over one end of our bed, while on the other end Morgan gazes wonderingly at the shiny pages of a decorating magazine. "And here's the second and third floor. Okay, now, here's the laundry."

She points at one corner of the first floor. Just off the living room is a tightly designed little room where the pub once had its kitchen, with a cellar door for the kegs and a side door for deliveries of mutton, carrots, and potatoes.

"This old kitchen is now being used as a laundry," she says. "Which means there's no kitchen on the ground floor, which means . . . well, which means this is a very weird house. Right now they have the dining room and kitchen both up on the second floor. So the first thing we do is move the kitchen back down to where it was."

"Right."

"And that'll be easy, since we know there's already power and water in there. That's why they turned it into a laundry. And now, their current kitchen" – she hauls out more of her drawings – "is up on the second floor, where you'd normally have your bathroom and maybe a laundry room. So that's what we'll do there. We'll have the sink here, the toilet here, a wall along there, and washer and dryer *here* and *here*." She ticks off each spot with a pencil.

"How about a utility sink in there?" I suggest.

"Okay." She pencils in another mark. "A utility sink."

"Good."

"Or" – she taps her pencil on our future kitchen – "we could put the washer and dryer under the counter in the kitchen. That's what a lot of homes here do."

"Hmm."

"And now" – she points at the second floor again – "there's where they have the dining room and the fireplace."

"Where the floor is completely out of plumb?"

"Yes. That'll be the master bedroom. And the next room down, the den – that can become Morgan's room."

His floor is nearly as slanted as ours. The height of any one side of any room in this house will not quite match the height of any other side. For that matter, the stories themselves in old British homes never quite agree: you do not take the stairs up to a second floor, but rather to its general vicinity; the rooms and hallways will all have steps going up and down, and none of them add up. Imagine Escher drawing illustrations for Beatrix Potter. It's as if the artisans were making it all up as they went along; and considering how illiterate most people were back then, perhaps they were. One might also suspect that ale merchants did a steady business among builders.

"And here" – she lays out a last set of graph-paper drawings – "is the third floor. Three bedrooms right now. Those will be your office, my painting studio, and a guest room."

"I want the room with all the ivy in its window."

"That's every room in the *house*."

It's true. We ponder what to do with the ivy that is enveloping the exterior of the house; what to do about the exposed beams and radiators, and the piled-stone foundation in the basement; what to do with the four-hundred-year-old stairwell that is coming to pieces – the kind of things that no normal American homeowner faces. They don't even start from the same materials here. It's all stone, brick, plaster. Wooden houses are unheard of in Britain: one homeowner landed in the newspapers here recently with the revelation that his *freakish clapboard house* was proving impossible to mortgage; apparently, British insurers were fearful that a wolf might come along and blow it down.

But our house is British to the core: it is a brooding hulk dragged out of a quarry. And we get to fill it with new *stuff*. We pore over catalogs from Argos and Next Home, imagining a future lit by the cool glow of Euro-appliances. The manufacturers over here are all different: Beko washing machines, Indesit dryers, Britannia stoves. Jennifer and I enjoy pronouncing their names just for the sheer novelty of it. We are, for example, determined to get a new refrigerator by an Italian concern with the delightful name of Smeg. The Smeg of our dreams is a glorious rounded slab that looks as if it were carved out of the back end of a '57 Buick and colored in a primal Crayola palette: red, green, or blue. But best of all, when someone asks what you've been doing all morning, you can say, "Defrosting my Smeg."

Sometimes I imagine that we would like to hide our appliances and make the interior true to its time, but then I come to my senses. We really just want it to feel old without carrying the inconveniences of old age. Selective memory is a good thing for designers to have, for some home innovations are best forgotten. I don't much care for outhouses or lead pipes or for chasing after old nags to get horsehair for our plaster. And it gets worse, for *Manufacturers and Builders* magazine carried this arresting headline in its January 1892 issue:

Door Knobs, etc., from Blood and Sawdust

It is about a building material called *hemacite,* invented by one Dr. D. W. Dibble, from a pressurized combination of sawdust and cattle blood. The Dibble Manufacturing Company made everything from house trimmings and doorknobs to cash register keys and roller-skate wheels out of the stuff. Why, just imagine being in his workshop the day that Dr. Dibble, staring at a bucket of cow blood, suddenly sat up in his chair and said: *Hey, I think we can make doorknobs out of this.*

"Hemacite," notes the magazine, "is susceptible of a high polish, is impervious to heat, moisture, atmospherical changes, and, in fact, is practically indestructible." So hemacite house fixtures, strong and durable as they are, surely live on. The next time you find yourself running short on bouillon, consider boiling your doorknobs.

We have a kazoo from a children's set of musical toys. Morgan never showed any interest in it until last night, when he picked it out of a pile of neglected toys and began to buzz loudly upon it. But it is such a weedy, inferior-quality kazoo – that there could even be different qualities of kazoos is a strange notion, but there you have it – that this morning I go outside and push through a knot of book tourists. I must find a concert-quality kazoo. Alas, there are none to be found in a rural place like Hay. But . . .

"What is it that you are looking for?" the elderly clerk asks.

I gaze about the shop of F. W. Golesworthy & Sons. They are outfitters in a true sense – an old village store designed to fit you up for an outing, with a stock top-heavy with rain hats, wellies, tweed coats, walking sticks, and woolly socks.

"I need a duck call."

"Hmm, ah, yes. A duck call, yes."

He stoops down to rummage through the goods behind his counter. "Duck call, duck call," he mutters. He shifts aside boxes of compasses, bootlaces, and waterproofing kits and draws out a small parcel.

"There. One duck call. Ten pounds," he says.

I eagerly tear it out of its packaging as I leave the store and give it a mighty blast.

Kwaa kwaa! it braps into the air. *Kwaa! Kwaa!*

It is, the packaging informs me, an ACME Bird and Game Call, so it must be good, considering how great their giant anvils and jet-propelled skates are. I happily tuck it into my pocket and head back up Broad Street; then I notice a sign in Booth's shop window. They are closing at five-thirty now, instead of seven; the town's stores are changing over to their winter hours, with its drowsy days of drifting snow and taking inventory for the next bookselling season.

"Paul!"

I look up from the store notice; Booth is coming down the sidewalk toward me.

"I want your opinion."

"Oh. On what?"

"It's growing." He motions me inside his shop. "American literature. You know that there are other book towns too – there's one in Scotland, another in France, another in Germany . . . it is becoming a movement. But we must make it viable, profitable."

"One always hopes – "

"American literature. It is the key. I think a store in Scotland might do well with books on the American West. How do you think we might reach an arrangement with Rudy Giuliani?"

"With . . . what? For *Wild West* books?"

"A mayor's proclamation for our American literature section," he announces grandly, then immediately turns his attention elsewhere in the shop, leaving me to ponder ideas that he has, in the space of a few seconds, already concocted, proclaimed, discarded, and forgotten. He is now focused on a more serious concern: how to rid himself of Richard Branson's memoirs, which Booth has resorted to giving away free copies of with the purchase of any other book. There is some question as to whether this will attract customers into the shop or frighten them away.

I am waiting patiently in line at the Londis market with my Mullerice and a jar of bramble jam when I notice what the burly fellow in front of me is buying. It is a tin of – wait for it – *Mr. Brain's Pork Faggots.**

One hardly knows where to begin.

Grocery bag in hand, I stroll from the market over to Martin Like's office, with the same daily question yet again:

"The Sixpence building survey. Is it – "

"It's right here," he interrupts me.

"What?"

"I–it's here." He smiles and hands me a spiral-bound report. "I tried calling you several times today, but your line was engaged."

I flip through the pages quickly.

"Jennifer's going to be happy to see this. We're really ready to move in."

"Yes, w-well . . . I–I should read that survey carefully."

"Yeah, okay!" I bound out.

I admire the buildings about me as I walk home: the ivy-covered mass of Kilvert's, the leaning stones and moss of the old Baptist church, the solid stone of Pemberton's, the ancient plastered mass of Oscar's. And now we will be their neighbor.

"I've got the Sixpence survey!" I announce jubilantly as I arrive back at The Apartment.

* "In a Rich West Country Sauce." What, still not hungry?

"Yay! Let me see."

I fish the duck call out of my pocket to distract Morgan, and then Jennifer and I sit at the kitchen table to study the building report. It is a room-by-room dissection of the place, with page after page of evidentiary photos of cracks, sags, and rot. The old familiar words loom up at us: Beetles. Damp. Fungus. Foul water. Crazing. Decay . . .

Kwaa kwaa!

. . . Split joists. Light peeping through the roof. Water seeping into the cellar. Collapsing floors. A veritable museum of ancient wiring.

"Well." I shrug. "We sort of knew all this already."

"Hmm."

"What?"

"Look down here. This paragraph."

By the way . . . all the floors and walls will have to be torn out.

Kwaa!

Sixpence House turns out to need rather more than a new lick of paint. We have always lived in what we thought were old homes, places a century old or so. These are mere striplings next to the Sixpence, though. Sixpence House is a really old house, and like any truly old house it bulges, it crimps, it squats, it leaks and groans. But the slanted floor in the dining room, and the rolling shallow waves that the floorboards have deformed into, these are not merely old age. The house next door is *leaning* on the Sixpence, like a friendly drunk staggering around full of the old pub's pints of bitter.

"Oh my," Jennifer sighs.

"Oh," I repeat numbly. "My."

"What should we do?"

I drum my fingers on the table, considering.

Kwaa!

"I think . . . I will take out the recycling now."

"Okay."

I need a walk out to the recycling center just to clear my mind. As I leave the building, a distinct gray tint is in the air: smoke. A black spot flutters into my face and – puh! – I swat and spit it away, grasp it in my hand. When I open my palm, I see what it is: a charred scrap of paper. I look up and see other scraps fluttering down upon the smoky wind and into the gutters of Castle Street.

Ah. Someone is reducing their stock today.

I stride out into the whirling particles of ash. They don't pick up recycling here; you have to lug it several blocks over to the parking lot by the Tourist Information Center and feel your arms ache as you tip out your bagfuls of crossed-out manuscript pages, week-old copies of *Private Eye,* and dozens of empty All-American Taste Cola cans.

When I get to the Dumpster, I gaze over at the Hay School. It abuts the parking lot. Dozens of kids are on the playground, milling about, screaming, skipping, talking, bouncing balls; their combined voices are a sort of high-pitched white noise. They are all in their blue uniforms, and watching them makes me wonder whether Morgan will ever join them. I visualized him having something quaint and unusual that he could look back upon. And yet, he wouldn't know the difference, only I would: whatever place we move to, that's where he'll have his first memories, make his first friends, and living there will seem as natural as the sky above. Living anywhere else, to him, will be unthinkable. A whole series of decisions and indecisions and coincidences create the house that you are born into, but kids don't know. To them, it has Always Been This Way.

So we convene a household meeting. This is not difficult to arrange, given that I am home twenty-one hours a day. Being a writer means you don't have to commute and punch in; it is a profession that tends to attract housebound sorts in the first place. When I go out, it is usually in the afternoon, a strangely empty, quiet time in many towns. Everybody is at work except me.

I am happy when I am at home.

But we are not at home. The Apartment is nice, yes, but I am still living out of my suitcase, Jen out of her plaid bag, Morgan out of his stroller, and we are all going crazy. I want to be sequestered in my office, surrounded by a teetering stack of wormy old books; Jennifer wants to be spread out over the bed with her longhand manuscript pages, a jigsaw puzzle half-assembled on a nearby board; Morgan wants to be watching his Teletubbies videos while trick-riding on the handlebars of his rocking horse.

"We are ready for a house," Jennifer says.

"Yes."

"But not this one."

"No."

"It would cost a fortune to fix it."

"Mmm. We've already gone through a fortune just looking for a house."

"It's winter now. We'll have to wait till the spring before anything new comes on the market."

"Yeah."

There is a long silence.

"There's really no one our age in this neighborhood, either."

"I know."

Maybe parents don't belong here in the middle of town; they certainly don't belong in Sixpence House. It will be a glorious home someday, with enough love and money. But both are already fully accounted for in our household: we are a couple with a baby, and people with babies should not be in houses that need more attention than their child does. And we are, in any case, irredeemable city folk

195

in our attitude to such homes. The essayist Gail Hamilton nails it in her 1862 book, *Country Living and Country Thinking:*

> People who live in cities and move regularly every year from one good, finished, right-side-up house to another . . . have fallen into a way of looking upon a house only as an exaggerated trunk. We do things differently in the country. We live in a house until it cracks, and then we plaster it over; then it totters, and we prop it up; then it rocks, and we rope it down; then it sprawls, and we clamp it; then it crumbles, and we have a new underpinning, – but we keep living in it.

I found this book in Hay. I find everything in Hay, it seems, except a place to live.

"So now what do we do?" Jennifer says.

"I'd like to spend a little more time here."

"And then?"

"Go home, I guess. Someday."

Jennifer nods.

"Now," she says, "tell me where that is."

Chapter Eighteen
Arrives at the Wrong Time

I AM STANDING alone in the London hotel room that I have spent far too much on. It is getting unbearably hot. And I am red and burning already with embarrassment at myself in front of the full-length mirror. There is a reading at the ICA just a couple hours from now, one that I'm not even scheduled to read at, but that one of the writers asked if I wanted to read –

Do I want to read?

My book has not come out yet. I have never read in front of people before. Should I?

"Of course you should," Jennifer had said. "We're flying back next week. You might not get another chance before we leave the country."

And so I have been reading my papers over and over again aloud in front of the mirror, practicing each nuance, each gesture. I am horrible. I am reading like a marble-mouthed grad student at the most boring MLA panel imaginable.

I am the frog slowly being boiled. I do not know that the housekeeper has left the radiator all the way up, and so with each run-through, and then each page, I strip off a bit more clothing, until I am finally reciting in my underwear. I still sound terrible, and what is worse, now I can smell my own armpits.

Inevitably, horribly, night falls. The reading time is approaching. It is absolutely pissing down with rain outside. All the taxis are full, splashing at me as they roar by on Russell Street in the black, cold, slick night, until finally

— "ICA, down on the Mall," I tell him —

and off we swerve onto Bloomsbury, heading south. To keep them dry, my papers are crammed under my shivery thin jacket – all my winter clothes are still in storage in some Oakland warehouse; I thought I'd be settled into a home here by now – and as I regain feeling in my extremities, I rifle through my papers one more time, stupidly mouthing the awkward pages to myself like Luca Brasi preparing to meet the Godfather. Jammed in amongst my work is the ICA flyer for the event, which reads, simply:

Welcome to This Flyer

Which eschews the usual principles of flyers by not being so pretty to look at and quite detailed about the things you can expect to find at the event we are advertising.

And among the events it lists is this one:

Young Writers
Writing stories live, in front of you, while you drink.

But when I arrive, only a few people are milling around outside; inside, a DJ is stringing out thick ropes of cable. Nothing's happening. I am early. So I open my umbrella and step outside into the rain, which has abated a bit.

I meander aimlessly, with only a vague idea of where to find Piccadilly Circus. I walk down Pall Mall, and I am the only person there – not another human in sight; then through the royal gates, and up past a spectral building with a row of huge torches flaming and whipping in the wind out front. I stand beneath them and look around at the old stone buildings. A few besuited people inside look and stare out at the rain, not seeing me. I feel that I am in a dream, drifting in darkness.

Somewhere, just a couple meters under my feet, is a beautiful old sewer. I only know this because of a fine young reporter named John Hollingshead, who wrote a book called *London Underground* in 1862. Hollingshead, a grown man, did what we all only dreamed of when we were eight years old: he pulled on some hip waders, tossed aside a storm-drain grill, and ventured down to explore the gurgling, rat-infested sewers of London. This journey, bear in mind, was in an era before disinfectants, antibiotics, or Lava soap, back when sewers were rich in cholera and dysentery. Hollingshead ventured to explore the charmingly named King's Scholars' Pond Sewer; that way he avoided any blood sewers, which are the ones that ran under slaughterhouses and meat markets and abounded in rats; and also he wisely steered clear of the sewers below soap and tallow makers, which were stinking rivers of burning lye and deadly gas.

No, the sewers around Piccadilly and the Mall are altogether more pleasant:

> We peeped up an old red-bricked, long disused branch sewer, under some part of Mayfair, that was almost blocked to the roof with mountains of black, dry, earthy deposit . . . The bricks in this old Mayfair sewer were as rotten as gingerbread; you could have scooped them out with a spoon.

Hollingshead ventured on, even going underneath Buckingham Palace where, as the royal feces swirled about his feet, he bellowed patriotic songs. Imagine the expression of the ladies-in-waiting when they heard a ghostly "God Save the Queen" reverberating out of their drains.

I wander on, finally stumbling into Piccadilly, send an e-mail to my wife from the Tower Records, and grab a two-week-old *New York Times* – it is strange to read this, full as it is with predictions about the presidential election that happened a week ago, none of which prophesy the hanging chads or butterfly ballots that have frozen the gears of American government and have every European TV and radio pundit chortling that *perhaps we should send election observers over there, haw haw haw!* – and I make my way up to the second floor of the Burger King on Piccadilly, which, like the McDonald's in Times Square, has one of the best and cheapest views of the crowds below. Masses of tourists, taxis, and umbrellas jostle and flow like corpuscles.

And then I cannot find my way back. I walk the wrong way up Regent Street, huddling in the rain under the closed entrance of the Aquascutum shop, clumsily opening up a folding map and trying to figure out where I am. Having accomplished this, I proceed farther in the wrong direction, until I pass Oxford Street and know that I am certainly lost. Finally, I hail another taxi, and it takes me back again.

I am late; the ICA is packed now. Music is thudding off the walls and onto the floors, the bass tapping my rib cage. Everyone is smoking, drinking, and young; and you cannot get by without squeezing past asses and elbows. The reading has already started, and dammit, I am late late late, and a couple of bored-looking crew members with headsets are guarding the theater door, telling me:

"It's full."

"But the people reading tonight wanted me to . . . to . . . uh . . ."

And I stand there, some schmuck with a sheaf of paper, babbling.

They look at each other. "It's full."

I walk away, wander around, get nowhere. Understand: I hate this place. I am phobic of crowds. Not in an unreasoning way, for I don't mind crowded streets, or a few people in a small room, but I cannot bear it when a room of any size is packed with human bodies. And here I am, alone, in a room full of people whom I do not know, away for the night from wife and child for the first time ever, in the wrong country, and I am afraid of crowds and loud noises.

So.

There is only one place in the building where I can set down my umbrella, my dog-eared clutch of papers, and think in peace; that is, of course, the bathroom. The hoppers are blissfully quiet, uncrowded. But the toilet seat is hideous – oh, those ICA members have bad aim. I hang my umbrella on the toilet paper dispenser, tuck my papers under my arm, and lean against the side of the stall to read the *Times Book Review*. Much better. Inevitably, the toilet works its magical powers of suggestion. There's nowhere dry for me to put my papers down, so I have to tuck my papers under my chin while I pee, which works till – *chiff* – into the toilet, and I grab, and recoil, then grab again – and I have saved my manuscript, the thing I am still hoping to read from this evening, except for the first page, which is not just soaked, it is soaked with urine. I stand alone in the bathroom, horrified. I do not have another copy with me. But, what they do have here is – a hand dryer. And so there I stand, drying off my masterpiece over the ineffectual vent. It takes a long time. Someone finally walks in on my performance art, and there I am, drying my pee-soaked words – Hello, top of the evening to you. Finally I give up and throw the whole thing out.

And this, I guess, is the story of my first reading. I had built up the evening in my mind into . . . I don't know, something. And now I only have a rueful dread dripping into me: it is like all my evenings from adolescence onward until I met my wife, back when I was single and spent my evening hours reading and writing and listening to albums over and over, imagining that everyone was out in the thrilling night doing something with themselves, everyone but me; and whenever I was indeed doing something, I'd be paralyzed by doubt and regret afterward. It is a melancholy that I have rarely felt since. Christopher Morley ingested its slow-acting poison as well, and expressed it best in his book *John Mistletoe:* "Night, I have discovered, has a faintly bitter taste, caused by its large ingredient of Unattained Possibility."

I can hear the theater finally letting out for intermission, and an outrush of people come clattering into the bathroom. Time for me to leave my sanctuary.

Two computers have been set up, dueling PCs, and hooked into projectors to flash their screens jumbo-sized onto a nearby wall. Two authors are typing away, knocking out short stories while the crowd watches. Only, neither can really write much, because people keep wanting to talk to them. A few us actually face the projection on the wall, holding our beers and watching the words unfurl on the screen.

Unfurl is not the word: it implies textile fluidity and grace, like the snapping of a flag in the wind. This writing is not graceful. It is sputtering – a sentence, a clause, a couple of lines rip out, then the cursor hesitates, backfires, zips up a couple lines to fix a typo, but ignores another right next to it, then zips back down, sits and blinks and thinks and then g-r-i-n-d-s out a word or two, then sprints, then stops again, waggles back and forth, spits out a verb . . .

Writers were not always such a spectacle, were they? At least, not before Dickens, our first modern media star of literature, the first whose brilliance was spun out into simultaneous magazine editorships, lecture tours, dictionaries, product sponsorships, and book after book after serialized book until he dropped dead of exhaustion at age fifty-eight.

And now? Everyone wants something from the writers. But what? What can they really give here, other than their words and a few moments of friendly attention? *What do you want?* is the unspoken question you face when you approach a stranger. What do you want from these strangers? You do not know them. I am being published soon myself, though perhaps published and forgotten – "Ehhh," a writer muttered to me once as we drove through Philly, "we're both going to be footnotes. Maybe not even *that*" – and yet the boundary has been crossed. The people I have spent all my life analyzing and speaking about as if I understood them, I am becoming one of them and I understand now that I know nothing about them, that I know as little as one would about any other complete stranger whom one has never met.

I have been watching her writing for an hour.

"Shit!" she yells.

ILLEGAL OPERATION E4
THIS PROGRAM WILL SHUT DOWN
OK?

There is a gasp from the crowd, and my eyes turn to the top of the projected screen: *Untitled Document 1.*

An ICA staffer runs over to hover ineffectually and tap at the keyboard.

"I'm sorry," he finally says.

He does not add, *You should save your work more often,* which is good for him, because if he does say this, he will be pummeled by every writer in the building. For a moment we all just stand there, looking at the bit of text peering out from behind the blot of the OK button, which when pressed will destroy her story, and that is not really OK at all.

She glumly clicks the button; nothing happens. The computer is frozen.

"Oh, really," she mutters, and stalks away.

The staffer makes a few last hopeless keystrokes, shrugs, and reaches back to switch off the power strip. The story vanishes forever into the ether of 220 household current.

Writing gets destroyed all the time. Published writing is the most obvious victim. During the Reformation, ill-wishers used copies of Duns Scotus to wipe their bottoms; and if you are heartless enough to break open the spine of any nineteenth-century book and look inside, you will find it reinforced and lined with scrapped paper from some other, less successful book: last year's almanac, say, or the outdated catalog endpapers for Ticknor and Fields. Paper was too expensive not to reuse. In 1814, when one American printer gave up trying to print the porn novel *Fanny Hill,* another hapless printer bought the abandoned sheets and marbled over them to use inside the covers of his rather less flighty project on the just ended War of 1812: *Barbarities of the Enemy, Exposed in A Report of the Committee of the House of Representatives*. Only, the marbling didn't really take, and the text of *Fanny Hill* bled through, so that delighted readers could read *the naughty bits* inside the cover of their government report. The recycling process is more thorough these days; books that are absolute stiffs, too hopeless even for the remainder table, go to mills where they are torn to pieces with band saws and then pulped into raw paper, suitable for . . . well, toilet paper, actually.

But the loss of unpublished writing is the greater tragedy, of course. Ralph Ellison lost a whole manuscript in a fire, and Carlyle's history of the French Revolution was famously consigned to the hearth by his maid – maybe too famously, as that story always sounded suspiciously apocryphal to me. There is also deliberate destruction, which is regretted later. About ten years ago, I threw an entire handwritten novel manuscript into a trash bin outside the Wren Library, at the College of William and Mary. When I had second thoughts the next morning, the trash was gone. But you cannot have posthumous regrets or changes of heart, which makes wills even more dangerous to writing; Franz Kafka willed his executor, Max Brod, to burn all his manuscripts, a request that Brod quite fortunately disobeyed.

But I understand him. Along with all my other fears of dying, I lived in constant fear that somehow I would die before my book was finished, or before I'd revised it properly, and now I worry that I will die before I see it come out. It is a real concern. A friend of mine likes to press copies of a book called *Tuning the Rig* upon people – "But it's just a book about boating," they say to her, puzzled. But Harvey Oxenhorn's book is about boating the way that *Walden* is about hoeing beans, which is to say that it is not really about that at all; it is about a process of discovery that takes place while sailing in a tall ship to the Arctic. It is a wonderful book, and it almost wasn't published: first the editor that bought it quit his job, then the publisher was sold, the book was dropped, and then Oxenhorn himself was dropped by his agent. At each step *Tuning the Rig* might have disappeared forever, and I suppose it seemed miraculous when the book did finally come out. But now we will never know what else this book might have spawned. Oxenhorn was killed in a head-on auto collision the day after its publication.

To see any library, any bookstore, any archive, is like seeing a city:

you are viewing buildings constructed atop the unknown and unknowable cities that once were and once might have been.

Other books are not physically destroyed, but exist in a living death – doomed to never be reopened, reread, or reissued. Some have a perfectly good idea that is squandered on a perfectly bad writer. Take the 1956 memoir *The Glazier*. It is a son's account of his father, an uneducated and not terribly good glass artisan at the turn of the century who was determined to create art with his shaky family business and pressed his three rather unwilling sons into service as assistants. He was, the son says, "an expert in failure" – naïve when dealing with unscrupulous suppliers, simpleminded in his aesthetics, and stubbornly resistant to more modern yet less crafted methods of producing leaded glass. The opening of the book is heartbreaking: years later, long after the father has died, the son sits in his old London workshop. It is a fashionable little café now and bears no mark of its past occupants; but the son is choked up by the sight of the floorboards. Those remain: they are the very ones he and his father once trod upon. Between the cracks of these floorboards, he knows, are still wedged tiny crystals of cracked colored glass, fine as dust, scattered in when his clumsy and hapless father dropped a priceless load of just completed windowpanes.

It should have been a great book. In the right hands, it could have been an outright classic. But it isn't: the narrator is peevish and judgmental, and utterly unable to let his family's story speak for itself.

Then there are books that are not bad, but also not good enough. I have a book written by Helen Simpson, published in 1928, titled *Cups, Wands, & Swords*. I bought it thinking it was an ampersand-supernatural caper, like *Bell, Book & Candle*, or *Bedknobs & Broomsticks*. But it isn't; the reference to tarot is a first-chapter throwaway that bears the mark of a hasty addition made at the behest of a fad-addled editor. The book is an altogether more curious creature, the story of a Australian girl who moves to England to be nearer to her fraternal twin brother, a drama student at Oxford. The twins are emotionally incestuous, and the novel turns upon his apparent suicide after she gets married. It is promisingly dark material.

But Simpson failed. The sister is infuriatingly passive, the brother is an arrogant boor, and the book is full of brilliantly witty lines that somehow never add up to a conversation. Simpson was no slouch: two of her novels were adapted by Alfred Hitchcock into movies – the 1930 thriller *Murder!* and the 1949 outback drama *Under Capricorn*. But she is out of print now, and if this book is any indication, she will stay that way. It is a horrible dilemma; the frustrating thing about failed books by talented writers is that they have wonderful passages in them that will never be salvaged, never raised up from the watery depths of obscurity. The book's second chapter is a finely drawn portrait of the twins as nannied children, and could to stand up to anything by Katherine Mansfield; and later there is a perfect moment when the twin brother invites a group of strangers to a party: "The names, in order of arrival, were: Higginbotham, Rowbotham, Ramsbottom, Sidebottom, Winterbottom, Shufflebottom, and Botham-Wetham."

Simpson's finest passage comes shortly after the sister's arrival in Oxford:

"Tony, aren't things ever what one thinks?"

"Depends on what one has thought."

"Yes, but – you wouldn't believe how silly I was about England. I thought the people wouldn't even be made of the same stuff. I thought the earth wouldn't just be earth. Oh, I don't know – "

She sought and found an instance.

"Like this place. You said you had digs in an eighteenth century house. And I'd thought about it. And this is it. Don't you see – ?"

She broke off, and he answered, not her words but her meaning:

"Yes, but you know what you've been doing; filling in the picture too much. Too many details. Eighteenth century; that makes you think of laced coats, and coaches and masks, and candles, and chambermaids tripping about in mob caps. That's what, underneath, you were expecting. You're shocked by the carpet, and Annie in a pink silk jumper. But that's only surface. When you're more used to England you'll get the feeling of the centuries coming through it all."

Over seventy years have passed, and the new era that so jarred upon her is now itself a part of the lost nostalgic past, the stuff of Waugh and Wodehouse and *Masterpiece Theatre*. But her complaint is as true today as it was then; and so is her brother's answer. Any visitor to Britain today could identify with the sentiment in this passage. But they won't. The book is for all purposes lost, and it was buried by its own author.

Simpson was an Australian immigrant to Britain herself. Even back then, the longing was setting in, the feeling of having shown up too late for the party. Americans do not know nostalgia for their country in the ways that Britons do, for they have not yet lost more than they have gained. My parents were part of a wave of expatriation from a crumbling empire; even now, my relatives cannot comprehend why I would want to move *to* Britain. How many Americans leave America, as opposed to those coming in?

Even now, the fraction must be minuscule. And has it ever been much different? How many people willingly left Rome at its height, I wonder? Or London, a hundred years ago? Empires have their own gravitational force, which inescapably pulls all objects toward their core. And then, when their mass is spent, the objects float away.

Someday, when the United States is a has-been, then we too shall know that indescribable British feeling; except that then it will be known as that indescribable American feeling. It is the sensation of being a fat bag of sand with a little hole in the bottom, slowly draining out. It has become impossible to live over here without being reminded of a past that is palpably gone: it creeps over you in the most ludicrously inconspicuous places.

Many British homes, for instance, have an electric fire in the living room. It is becoming harder to find a house in Britain that has not replaced its beautiful old wood- and coal-burning fireplace with the alleged improvement of an electrical heater, typically in the misbegotten shape of a faux fireplace. The shape only serves to remind you of what you manifestly do not have, which is a crackling wood fire on a cold winter's night. These hideous appliances are the bane of British decor; no matter how beautiful your tables and chairs, how carefully selected your wallpaper – you still have that ugly *contraption* glowing at you from the middle of the room.

There is no denying that the old heating methods were inferior, and the British were not sad to see them go. An *Illustrated London News* from January 1929 was hailing electric "Magicoal" fireplaces as the heat wave of the future in council flats and stately manors alike, for "they convey a wonderful sense of comfort, and at the same time enhance the beauty of furnishings and decorations."

It's nice to think so. I am glad that people are staying warmer now.

The electric heaters are certainly better than the comically stingy coin-operated gas heaters you still find in some old flats. And yet, when I see the modern electrical faceplate of Britain . . . like Helen Simpson, like every generation that comes to these shores, I feel an unfathomable regret that I have arrived one era too late.

stet stet stet stet stet stet stet stet stet stet stet stet stet stet stet stet

stet   stet

stet   Chapter Nineteen   stet

stet   stet

stet stet stet stet stet stet stet stet stet stet stet stet stet stet stet stet

IT IS WAITING for me when I get back. I open the FedEx package, and out it flops: my *Banvard's Folly* manuscript. A note drifts out of the box, explaining: Here is the proofed manuscript. Proofreader corrections are in red; flagged pages have questions and changes for you to attend to. If you do not want the proofreader's changes to be used, mark it *stet* in a different-color pencil.

Please don't lose this manuscript, the note pleads.

Morgan toddles over and seizes the bubble wrap that the manuscript is wrapped in; he snaps each bubble with a fascinated glee, and I join him for a while. Then I finally pull the manuscript out of its deflated jacket. It is four months worse for wear and bristling with little Post-it flags, scrawled over with proofreader's comments and penned-in notations from at least two editors. Every page has several corrections or questions, which means that there are a total of . . . I don't know, a thousand?

"When one hears of a publisher being shot by an author," the *Illustrated London News* columnist James Payn wrote in 1893, "it is well to have all the facts before us before expressing disapprobation."

The war between the publisher and the published is an ancient and honorable one; both sides are convinced, usually correctly, that the other does not know what it is doing. For the author, the sight of one's own proofed manuscript is shocking: when you have not read your own book in many months, opening it anew is like reading someone else's book. First you are curious about what it was that you wrote in the first place. Then you get curious about what they wrote in response. Then you get angry, then humbled. And then you get angry again. Then you lie in bed for a couple hours and sigh.

Once that's done, you get to work. And so I walk over to Oscar's, hoping to get my usual upstairs table by the window. But they've closed early for winter hours. I go to the Penny Bun; they're closed too. Then to The Granary; they are closed. The British are fond of closing their shops. I pace the sidewalk between The Granary and the town pay phone. I note, to no particular purpose, that the BT pay phone on Broad Street is the only pay phone in the country not papered over with tart cards, those poorly photocopied advertisements for local prostitutes that wittily note *Actual Photo* beneath some bosomy clipping out of a porn magazine.

The British can be ruthless promoters. One north-country churchyard used to have the following epitaph:

Sacred to the memory of JOHN ROBERTS,
stonemason and tomb-cutter,
who died on Saturday, October the 8th, 1800.
N.B. the business carried on by the widow, at No. 1, Freshfield Place.

In 1862, the London ad exec William Smith published a visionary little book called *Advertise. How? Where? When?* In it, he recalls when the Adelphi Theatre hired him to publicize a new play, and he printed up ten million promotional adhesive labels bearing the play's title. Jokers found quick use for the labels on unsuspecting passersby, and soon Mr. Smith was receiving indignant letters:

My husband went out last evening to a public dinner, and when he returned home at twenty minutes to two, *perfectly sober,* I found on his best dress-coat a piece of paper pasted on with the words **The Dead Heart,** and three on the inside of his hat. I am surprised to see your sanctioning such proceedings.

But more often British advertising has jarring and strangely melancholic notes to American ears; right now a print ad by the British Sausage Association features a bloodcurdlingly obscene close-up of plump, grayish-red sausages glistening with fat. It's enough to make a nun faint. And in a 1963 issue of *The Observer* magazine is a picture of four mascaraed Swinging Sixties birds crowded into a tiny London flat:

happiness is egg-shaped
ask any of the new-breed girls

The shorter the skirt, the less ironing. The straighter the hair, the less combing. The quicker the food, the nicer. The bigger the surplus of boys (and males now outnumber the females in the under-25s), the better. Life's here to be enjoyed. In this paradise of a world, breakfast usually means – quick! – eggs. Eggs are nice. Eggs keep you going longer and feeling brighter longer, not flagging, nibbling nor moaning mid-morning.

In ten years' time, when they've got twelve children between them, what then? Will their skirts and their spirits droop? Let us hope not. Let us wish them mornings as bright as those they now enjoy, and trust they have the wisdom to always *go to work on an egg.*

No American advertiser would ever think of selling food to the eighteen-to-twenty-nine demographic by reminding them, with a pensive little sigh, of *how miserable they might be in ten years*. But it is a testament to the British truthfulness. After all, eggs are indeed nice.

Curiously, the "go to work on an egg" tag line was penned by Fay Weldon, now a saleswoman at Bulgari. There is a real danger to writers who moonlight as ad copywriters that their sideline work will outlast their "real" work. The poet Lew Welch might have been mortified to know that, while few Americans can recite a line of his poetry, he has achieved literary immortality through this koan-like ad slogan: *"Raid kills bugs dead."*

If I am going to work on my manuscript in an establishment, it will have to be in the smoky confines of a pub. But then, I spy something just across the road: an empty pub called The Hogshead. I will have it all to myself. Success!

I step down from the sidewalk and into the dark interior. The Hogshead is just about the oldest free house – that is, a pub not run by a brewery – in all of Wales, and its tiny interior looks it. The wood is dark, the floors and walls and ceiling are dark, the air itself is dark. A coal fire is slowly dying in a corner grate.

"Oh," says a small voice. "I was just about to close."

I turn to the little bar; an elderly woman is smiling at me.

"I'm sorry. I can head out . . ."

"No, no." She waves me to one of the three little tables crammed onto the stone floor. "Sit down."

Now I feel bad for keeping her here. I glance outside; it is starting to rain. I suppose I should stay in.

"Okay," I oblige. "Please don't mind me. I'm just going to do a little work on my, uh, manuscript."

"Good. What can I get for you?"

"A cider?"

"What kind?"

"Um . . ." I try to remember what kinds there are. "Scrumpy?" I don't know what it is, but it sounds innocuous enough.

"We have excellent scrumpy."

She draws a pint from a barrel by the bar and sets the yellowish glass next my manuscript. Then she sits directly across the little table from me.

"Uh . . ."

"Don't worry about me. I won't interrupt your work."

I look about and see that her chair is the one closest to the hearth. I can hardly object to an old woman keeping herself warm on a miserable cold day.

"Um. Okay."

I start quietly reading my manuscript:

Peruse the documents of any era . . .

"So where are you from?"

I look up. "Sorry?"

"Where are you from?"

"San Francisco." I smile, then look back down.

Peruse the documents o . . .

"How's that?"

. . . any . . .

"What?"

"San Francisco. How is it?"

"It's nice. I like it."

Peruse the . . .

"Does it rain a lot there?"

. . . docu . . .

"Yeah, yeah. It does. Very British climate."

"Is it now?"

"Mmm hmm."

Peruse t . . .

"How's the cider?"

"Hmm?"

"The cider. How's your cider?"

"Oh, it's good."

"But you haven't had any."

"I . . . oh. Sorry."

I raise the glass up – "Cheers" – and take a swallow.

Oh god.

I feel my cheeks, my tongue, the skin on my head, shriveling and puckering. It is cider that I am drinking. Or rather, it was. But now . . .

"How is it?"

I am holding it in my mouth.

And . . .

then . . .

I . . .

swallow.

"Oh." I grit and smile. "It's good."

"It's very good cider."

I smile and nod. Tears are about to come to my eyes.

"Excuse me." She stands up. "Have to attend to something. I'll be right back."

She walks slowly into the back storeroom of the pub, and I frantically pick up my glass and look about the bar. Where can I tip my cider out? There is no sink here. My gaze falls upon the coal fire; no, this stuff might make it explode. Or worse, make it go out, and what kind of cad puts out an old woman's hearth?

And in a horrifying moment, I recollect why I have heard of The Hogshead before. A local merchant was telling me about it: "That singer fellow . . . what's his name? . . . Robert Plant . . . he went in there during the Hay Festival and bought a drink. Left it half-finished. So old Violet marched him back into the pub and wouldn't let him leave till he drank it. And he did, too."

"I'm coming right back," she calls from the storeroom.

Quick, quick, *think*. Dammit. I notice the little drain built into the bar countertop, meant to catch the tap drippings. I nearly tip my glass in, but, no, they're much too shallow, and anyway they're empty; she'll notice them full and know what I've done. I look to the door – it's raining, the ground is wet, I could open the door and toss it onto the sidewalk . . .

"I'm coming!" Shuffle shuffle. I leap back into my chair.

She looks at my glass as she comes back in.

"Aren't you going to drink your cider?" she asks.

I mope into Booth's with my wet backpack full of the priceless manuscript. I have proofed exactly one paragraph in the last hour.

Booth is at the counter, watching as Sid zips open a box of books with a carpet cutter. The King of Hay then peers at me through his thick lenses.

"Hello. You look thunderstruck."

I gaze at him woefully. "I have had an entire glass of Violet's cider."

"Capital stuff."

"Oh, yes." I am not sure, but I think I can hear Sid laughing under his breath.

"Have you found a house yet?" Booth asks.

"Still looking."

I haven't told anyone yet that we are leaving; somehow it feels like admitting defeat. Jennifer and I have settled on moving to Oregon, though we almost chose Vermont instead. For both states are like us – quiet, cheap, and liberal.

"You know," Booth says, "there's a retail space opening up next door."

"The one that had the living room set up in the window?"

"I'm thinking of expanding into it. Maybe have an American section."

"Really?"

"And I'd need a fellow to run it."

This takes a moment to sink in. "Oh . . . uh, I don't know . . ."

"You wouldn't want to?"

"No, no, I would . . . I just, I haven't any plans right now."

"Well, think about it."

I know that it is too late to stay now.

"Yeah, I will think about it," I promise. "Thank you."

Booth will have little trouble finding someone else to take my place. There are always more booksellers coming to Hay; they are tourists who never leave, who decide to stay and set up shop for themselves. Booth, never one to miss an opportunity to unload some books, has a sign up in his shop:

Start Your Own Bookstore!
Kits from £500

Every now and then, someone takes him up on it.

The first time I came to Hay, I was drawn into a low-slung building in the Back Fold by a sign proclaiming VICTORIAN BOOK-SHOP; and as I crouched behind a bookcase, I heard the owner talking with what I gathered was a neighboring bookseller:

"D'you see the new one that opened last week?"

"I did. The usual rubbish."

They both had a good laugh at this.

"It's Booth, you know. Tells every plonker who comes along that they can sell books, and pawns off a pile of junk on them for five hundred quid."

"Can't last."

"No. That's for sure."

I can't ask the store owner if he or his friend still hold the same opinion today. It's three years later, and now the Victorian Bookshop is closed.

But Booth is still open.

Bookstores do stumble and disappear. Geoffrey Aspin, a retired literature professor who ran a shop under the castle's shadow for over twenty years, now has nothing in his display but a hand-lettered sign bidding his customers farewell. But more often, it is the local businesses that are getting cleared away, swept aside by the rising tide of bibliophilic outsiders. Earlier this month it was the Davies grocery on Bear Street. Its emptied space, no longer displaying bread and bananas in the window, will probably reemerge in a month or two as a boutique or another bookstore. If it is the latter, it will be the town's forty-first.

Given a generation or two, these business too will become truly local. But for now, at least, there are no booksellers actually from Hay . . . with one exception. His name is Derek Addyman.

I walk down the street from Booth's and into Derek Addyman's orderly and tightly packed shop, and I slump onto the sofa that he keeps upstairs in the bookstacks. I'd said I'd be stopping by, and he is pausing to set some heavy folio volumes straight. Derek is a trim, amiable fellow in his forties and does not look like an antiquarian seller, which is to say that he wears blue jeans, but does not wear bifocals. It is to say he does not have any space not filled with books, but he does have a wife and kids. It is to say that he does not have hair in his ears, but he does have it on his head.

Rain is tapping at the window, and Booth's offer is still ringing in my ears. It makes me curious how Derek got his start.

"I started," he says, "by being born here. In a house about two hundred yards from this shop. My father and uncles were builders, and after I'd done that for a summer or two when I was sixteen or seventeen, I knew" – he pauses and sighs – "I didn't want to keep doing that, breaking my back out in the sun, when I was thirty."

"I guess books would be as far as you could get from that."

"Not exactly. They *are* heavy. But I didn't come to books immediately. I was in Hay in the summer of '76, unemployed, no idea of what I was going to do with my life. So I got a job with Booth."

"Really? You started with Booth?"

"Most people do. He's always hiring. The funny thing is, I wasn't much of a reader when I was younger. But you get pulled in, in a field like this."

The way Addyman tells it, Booth had him as his local lad, a strong back to move piles of books around. I think about the teenage Paul working in the Booth warehouse with me. Outsiders are booksellers; locals are bookhaulers.

"That's it." Derek nods. "I spent six months in the Hay Cinema shop doing nothing but moving stacks of books upstairs, moving books downstairs, moving books I'd already moved upstairs back downstairs again. You know how Booth is. And that summer, those book storage sheds were like saunas. At one point Richard brought over six or eight containers full of remainders from the States, and I was out there unloading them, with sweat just pouring out of me."

I remember that summer. I was over here for it. I was desperate to see some tanks and planes, so my aunt and uncle took me to the Aldershot to see the army display; they almost passed out from the heat. It's rare that Her Majesty's armed services create such a thrill any more. Recently, to save money, Royal Navy gunners were told to stop using shells for target practice and instead to yell *"Bang!"* Which is a very civilized way to fight a war, don't you think?

"Anyway," Addyman says, "one day Booth takes me aside, points at a stack of about a thousand books, and says, 'Right, Derek, price those.' And I looked at them, good God. But I went about doing it. And when I was done, he picked up twenty books or so at random and said, 'That's the right price. That's right. That one's wrong' – and so on, one by one. When he was done, he told me to shelve them."

And this, in Hay, is when you know that you have entered the trade.

"So you worked up from there."

"Slowly, yes. I was responsible for all kinds of books. Turnover was about one hundred per cent at the Cinema shop, maybe three hundred or four hundred thousand a year. Which means that, in ten years there, I handled three or four million books. Unbelievable. The strangest thing was that I was in charge of languages – you know, books in foreign tongues. And I couldn't read any of them."

"How on earth did you price them?"

"How? By thickness. I'm serious. You do it by weight. And how common or unusual a language is. A book in Mandarin Chinese? Common. A book in Hawaiian, that will cost you more."

Done shelving, he finally sits down.

"You know" – he hesitates – "we had a domestic tip – *dump* is the American word, isn't it? – just outside town, open until a few years ago. That tip was very . . ." He searches for a diplomatic word.

"Literate?"

"Yes. It was very literate indeed. I mean, some of the things at Booth just . . . could . . . not . . . move. Ever. Especially theology. And he'd get these collections of books – you have to understand, he's had some very strange people on his staff over the years, and their book purchases reflect that. And the other staff would have to deal with it. When I first started, we had one fellow who would just throw out entire theology shelves. Massive old leatherbound Bibles and the like – 'This won't sell.' – voosh." Derek makes a throwing motion over his shoulder. "I can only imagine what wound up in that tip."

A hint of a smile passes over his face. "Perhaps the Tree of Knowledge will grow on it."

I venture over to the Blue Boar, thinking I might find a table to work there; but I am out of luck. It is cold out and I am getting wet; I may as well go home and work there. I sigh and stroll back down Castle Street.

There is, at the far end of Castle Street, one bookshop perched on the corner. I stop in front of it and look into its window. The store is called Bookends, and it is aptly named, for they deal largely in remainders: it is indeed the end for these books. One time they did a sale where you paid a set price for books by the basket, paying by the pound, in effect, just as you would for a sack of potatoes or a trailerload of bauxite.

I heft up my backpack, and my manuscript moves, shifting from one side to the other. I have avoided going into this store for my entire stay here. I used to buy remaindered books fairly often, happy to get a bargain, but now it is just too disheartening to think upon. There is, to any author, something deeply melancholy about the remainder table in a bookstore. Every title, every name, every jacket – all you can see is your own book there. The ways to the remainder table are so many that they are beyond reckoning. A few well-placed pans by critics; getting scooped by another author who wrote a better book on the same subject; a trend that ended right before you arrived; a sloppy marketing campaign; a lousy jacket; a poorly chosen title; the misplaced optimism of a large print run.

Sometimes, people just won't *buy* the damn things.

One curious feature of the British literary landscape is that the newspapers here not only publish best-seller rankings, they also publish how many copies each book has sold. It can make for grim reading when you see just how few copies this translates to. A newly published poet can sell in the single digits almost every week and still make it into the top ten of new poetry for the year. Sometimes publishers are not keen on this information being made public; Little Brown spent £400,000 on the autobiography of Anthea Turner – she is the sort of smiling nonentity that occasionally becomes mystifyingly famous – and was then galled to see it publicly revealed that it sold only 451 copies in its first week. They didn't release her sales figures after that.

But the remainder tables do not lie; it is only a matter of time before she lands here. A few times publishers have tried to invert this problem and attempt to shame the public into buying. In 1937 Chatto & Windus ran ads for Peter Keenagh's *Mosquito Coast* with this scolding headline:

Only 271 Copies Sold!

A bit of information that the author was, no doubt, absolutely delighted to see revealed to the entire world. Doubleday tried the same approach in 1967 in America with Lawrence O'Sullivan's *An*

Hour After Requiem and Other Stories, complaining under the head-line THE UNRECOGNIZED LITERARY GENIUS that the book had sold less than two thousand copies, and that the author was having to support himself as an English tutor in a tiny apartment in Italy. Which is strange, considering that it amounts to an admission by the publisher that:

1. They didn't pay him very well, and
2. They don't know how to sell him either.

Perhaps the truth-in-advertising laws were stricter back then.

O'Sullivan flopped in spite of praise from Malcolm Cowley and Philip Roth. But then, so many remainders have lovely blurbs on the back. Not that this is a guarantee of quality: earlier this morning, Jennifer was reading a book that bore a blurb from the *Times* describing it as "luminous" – and indeed it would be, if you soaked it in kerosene and burned it.

I had watched her stifle a yawn. "Are you feeling that you are in the presence of luminescence?"

"No."

"What's it about?"

"A landscaper. Or something."

"Let me see the author picture." Hmm. "Is it," I ventured, "about coming of – "

" – age in the sixties," she sighs. "Yes."

"And divorce in the seventies? And midlife crisis and spiritual yearning in the eighties and nineties?"

"Oh yes. Oh my yes."

But here I am, late in the day, out in front of this unlit store of dead books, and that one is not in the window. But guess what is? *Motherless Brooklyn.* How can such things be? Where is the justice in that? I just want to go home, lie in bed listening to the radio, and let Morgan fling the pages of manuscript around the room.

And so I do. The revisions go okay, I guess, though sometimes in my manuscript there is open snapping between proofreader and author:

I do not think readers will get this reference.
MY readers will get it. STET.

Next Christmas, I have decided, I am going to buy all my writer friends the same present: green inkpads, and rubber stamps that read STET.

Morgan scribbles crayons over his stack of paper as I scribble green pencil notations over mine. The radio mutters on from the night-stand; it is good company. But I cannot really trust the radio here. This is because, you see, the British continue to insist on *trying to forecast their weather*. A more pathetic and humorous endeavor can hardly be imagined. It resembles nothing so much as sandpipers on the beach, running out onto the wet sand and then scurrying back in shock when a wave comes pounding down at them – over and over. Forecasters here must live in this same permanent state of amnesia; for if there was ever a country that deserves the gloriously nonsensical forecast "winds light to variable," that country is Great Britain.

But there is one art at which British radio has it all over the Americans. Occasionally you will hear commentators in America imply that the Golden Age of wireless is long gone, the fine old radio dramas of yore all swept away by TV, and now only available as mail-order tape sets of Bob & Ray. But radio drama never died. It just moved – to Bournemouth, I think. There, in a little bungalow, live dozens of octogenarian radio writers, and when they get cross, they take their teeth out and break sound-effects LPs over each other's heads. And then they sit down at their Underwoods and bang out another script of *The Archers*, a fifteen-minute radio series that first started running back when the country was still composed of molten lava.

More curious still is the long-standing resistance of the BBC to hiring any foreign actors. It is something of a sport to guess just which part of Sussex or Epping Forest a BBC "Egyptian" or "Frenchman" is from. While listening to Radio 4 today, I was treated to readings of American writers by one such distinguished actor. He delivered renderings of David Sedaris, Norman Mailer, and P. J. O'Rourke, all in precisely the same accent – a bizarre amalgam of Woody Allen and the Bowery Boys, with a few *dese* and *dose* thrown in for good effect. The result is that now a sizable portion of the Radio 4 audience believes that David Sedaris is, in fact, a bullet-headed longshoreman.

This is because there is only one type of American: brassy, boastful, and twenty decibels louder than anyone else in the room. That, at least, is what you will learn when you watch the British portray Americans. The effect is like watching a drag queen, in that queens do not resemble actual women so much as they resemble the caricature of women that men carry in their heads. British television eventually roused itself to make a star of one actual American: Ruby Wax, who is as famous here as she is unknown in her native country. And what is Ruby Wax like? Well . . . brassy, boastful, and twenty decibels louder than anyone else in the room.

Once Morgan has been put to bed I snap off the radio, toss aside my manuscript, and decide to calm myself with an old book. The books in our bedroom are now in stacks that are nearly waist high; but my favorite one is always on the nightstand. It is called *Recreations of a Country Parson,* published anonymously in 1861. The author,

Andrew Boyd, was a reverend's son from Glasgow who gave up law to become a minister himself. His book consists of what amount to pleasant musings upon the home, upon books, upon city and country life.

They are sermons in disguise, really, and they will put you to sleep. I mean that as a compliment: he is a calming writer. Boyd has an amiable voice that you would imagine the best sort of clergyman possessing. He is a companionable fellow, neither dogmatic nor uncommitted, and keenly aware of the absurdities of our world and of our human nature. He can be long-winded, and yet he has a beautiful essay on the detached and otherworldly sensation of taking a long railway ride early on a winter morning, before the sun has risen; and an even more subtle one on the charms of reading how-to books about things that one will never do. He treasures a volume on building beautiful homes, for example, purely for what he can vicariously imagine through it:

Therein lies the salt of such a book. The enjoyment of all things beyond eating and drinking arises out of our idealizing them. Do you think a child who will spend an hour delightedly in galloping round the garden on his horse, which is a stick, regards that stick as a mere bit of wood? No: that stick is to him instinct with imaginings of a pony pattering feet and shaggy mane, and erect little ears. It is not so long since the writer was accustomed to ride on horseback in that inexpensive fashion, but what he can remember all that the stick was; and remember too how sometimes fancy would flag, the idealizing power break down, and from being a horse the stick became merely a stick, a dull, wearisome, stupid thing. And of what little things imagination, thus elevating and enchanting them, can make how much!

Even more than when he wrote these words, our cookbooks and how-to books have taken on this characteristic. We may not use them, but buy them because it is pleasant to imagine how we might use them.

I am unaccountably fond of Boyd's little book. *Recreations of a Country Parson* was popular on both sides of the Atlantic in 1860s, and it went through numerous editions and two sequels. I doubt that it will ever get published again, though. No scholar will ever bother to write about Andrew Boyd, either. We like our meat of a stronger taste today, and *a classic that will put you to sleep* is not considered a ringing endorsement for book jackets. We shall not see its mild-mannered like again. If anyone did publish it today, I suppose it would wind up on the remainder table.

The Last Chapter
Ends with a Subtle Hint of
Further Mishaps in the Future

MY AMERICAN passport is missing.

"Stop worrying," I tell Jennifer. "I can get back into the country without the passport."

"No, you can't."

"I'll travel on my British passport. I'll be a tourist. A tourist to America! Then after I get in, I'll go to the passport office and get my new American passport."

"I don't know," she sighs. "Did you look everywhere?"

"Everywhere. Our tickets are for two days from now. I couldn't get a new passport in that time if I tried."

"Well, okay," she says doubtfully.

The most important thing to do before we leave, I decide, is to stock up on candy over at H. R. Grant & Son. Candy is in my blood; my father is an engineering consultant in cocoa processing, having designed and built factories for decades. My childhood was filled with watching him work at a drafting board in an office filled with back issues of *Manufacturing Confectioner,* Grainger catalogs, stacks of test molds, and assorted machined bits and pieces imported from Germany of whatever tempering machine or soft-center injection line he was working on that month. We would have massive raw blocks of chocolate sitting on pallets out in the garage, the results of test runs for his clients; my best friend and I would sneak out there with a hammer and chisel to smash off fist-size chunks.

I never saw my dad eat an entire piece of candy. Sometimes he would check a sample by nibbling off a corner and rolling the sliver about in his mouth; often he could tell you what country the cocoa beans had come from. But then he would throw the rest of the piece away uneaten. All our lives, my mother and I thought he didn't actually care much for the stuff he made.

"I *love* chocolate," he told us both one day, when he was about sixty.

My mother and I looked at him, dumbstruck.

"That's why I can't eat it," he explained. "I'm around it all the time."

I can vouch for this danger. My first job out of college was in a See's Candies store, where I gained about ten pounds in a month – as did all my roommates. But my real love for chocolate started at least ten years before that, back when I spent childhood summers in Britain with my relatives in Reading. To put this in context, it's like a Brit sending their child three thousand miles to spend two months in Hoboken. The primary effect of these trips was to instill in me a lifelong fear of Sainsbury's salad cream and orange barley squash. But one year I got sent over early and spent part of my sixth-grade education attending Emmer Green Primary School. My clearest memory of Emmer Green is that they crammed you full of incredibly stout food at lunchtime: steaming gravied platefuls of roast beef, and thick-lipped white bowls filled with prunes and hot custard. The classroom was no less bewildering; for one thing, my English classmates were years ahead of me in mathematics, already doing trigonometry, and yet they were curiously unconcerned about grammar lessons. They would read books and poetry, true, but in all my months there I never saw anyone open the grammar books stacked up in one corner under a poster of C. S. Lewis. But the students were not so diffident about other languages – they'd taken French since kindergarten.

My French teacher quickly gave up on trying to pare down my monumental store of American ignorance and would look the other way when I didn't show up to class. Instead, I'd sneak out of the school and down a hedge lane to the corner shop, and spend my precious 10p pieces on onion-flavored crisps, supersugared Irn-Bru soda, and ice cream cones with a candy bar jammed into them – the *Flake*. The Flake is the height of British candy technology; it is layers of randomly laid wavy sheets of chocolate molded into a bar. They melt in your mouth and crumble apart layer by layer if you grasp them too hard, resulting in telltale brown specks all over your clothes. They are really good – as is all British candy. When I got back to America and bit into a Hershey's bar, I nearly spat it out; it tasted as if it were covered in wax. What, I asked my dad, was going on here?

"They process chocolate differently over there. Higher carmelization, higher fat content."

"Why?"

"Well now," he explained, leaning back a little, "the formulation of American candy is driven by vendors in the South and West, where it's eighty, ninety degrees all the time, and pretty soon you have a mess. So you try to stabilize your chocolate and you lower the fat content. That's part of it."

"And they don't have that problem in England?"

"Of course not. It's fifty bloody degrees all the time."

The ironic thing is that, when you buy a candy bar at a vending machine on a British railway platform, it is *really* cold. If you want a modern refrigerator for your vending machine, my father once explained, you don't go to Europe – you go to New Jersey. American vending machines are cooled just enough to keep the candy from melting, and not a jot more. But British machines have gloriously inefficient and primitive refrigeration systems; I believe a typical one involves a team of urchins on a treadmill, a bellows, and an open vat of Freon. Their vending machines, bless them, are damned cold. And as any college student with a pound bag of M&M's stashed in the freezer knows, this is the best way to eat chocolate.

So I am off to stock up on good candy with a low melting point: Aeros, Yorkies, and the kind of massive Milkybar so big that you can smash walnuts with it. Other candies I simply enjoy buying for the wrapper, like the Nestlé Lion bar. Most manufacturers, when redesigning their product packaging, pare away the old slogans before adding new ones. This is why Phillips' Milk of Magnesia doesn't say "Relieves the Vapours; a Palliative for Womanly Hysteria." But Nestlé has made the Lion bar a veritable museum of sloganry:

Caramel, Filled Wafer, Crisp Cereal, Covered in Milk Chocolate
New Size – Now 25p
Wrestle a Lion – It's a Beast of a Bar
The Beast of a Bar With the Great Taste of Nestlé Chocolate

Count the rings in the chocolate coating, and you can see how many years each successive Nestlé copywriter lived.

I head up Castle Street, and each step I take feels a little heavy: this is last time I will be walking these streets as a resident. Dobson is standing out in front of the pharmacy.

"Still here?" he jokes. "Good heavens, how cold does it have to get to drive you Americans out?"

"Actually . . . we're leaving tomorrow."

"I'm sorry to hear that. You are coming back?"

"Oh, we always do."

"Yes." He squints up at the winter sun. "It's that kind of town."

Dobson shifts on his feet, so that he is standing directly beneath the pharmacy's large promotional sign for Wella hair conditioner, his body filling in the precise spot where the enlarged bottle would be. The sans serif ad copy floats above his head.

Derek Addyman walks by, then stops and gazes at him.

"Dobson is your introductory price just two pounds ninety-nine?"

"Yes," Dobson says. "And I've just been waiting for you to buy me."

"Are you indeed full of vitamin E?"

"I," Dobson says gravely, "am *bursting* with it."

I arrive at H. R. Grant & Son, ready to take in a heavy haul. But something is missing.

"Where's the candy gone?"

The owner sighs from behind the counter. "Ah," she says sadly, "we're leaving. Closing up."

"But, but . . . ," I sputter as I look around the little stationer's shop. "This shop is a hundred and fifty years old!"

"'Tis. I'll miss it." She gives a helpless shrug. The old businesses are going by the wayside, and there is nothing to be done about it.

In the afternoon the movers arrive. They are three men from Hereford, bearing flattened boxes, and we watch as they pack away our lives: our new, hopeful lives as loyal subjects of the crown, or of the local council at any rate – swaddled up in bubble wrap and brown tape, and jammed layer upon layer into the assembled multitude of boxes. The books, as always, are the problem here. One mover, a ringer for Bob Hoskins, sets down a stack of the books and shakes his head.

"We're running out of boxes for these books."

"Oh." I pick up a red-marbled volume of the *Edinburgh Chamber's Journal* from 1852. "Okay, I guess I have to start ditching some."

"Shouldn't be too hard in this town."

"No. It shouldn't."

He leaves with the last of the boxes, and Jennifer comes up the stairs with Morgan. Her expression is clouded over.

"Are you okay?"

"Yeah." She nods. "It's Diana."

"Oh, for god's . . . is this about the phone bill?"

"No, no." Jennifer sets Morgan down, and he rips off across the room. "She just came back from the doctor."

"Yeah?"

"Her breast. There's something there."

The air hangs heavy over us.

"What did the doctor say?"

"She's going to Cardiff tomorrow for a biopsy."

I let out a long exhalation.

"She's leaving before we'll have a chance to see her off," Jennifer adds. "You should stop by the store today."

No one wants my books. "We're well stocked," they all tell me, "because it's winter and there are no customers." I drop my box of books with a wallop out on the sidewalk in front of Pemberton's; my back hurts and I am not ready to carry them upstairs yet. You can leave a box of books out in the middle of the street in Hay, and no one gives it a second thought. I regard the box ruefully for a moment. Just what this town needs: more stranded books. *The New Yorker* once ran a cartoon, I think in the 1950s, showing a man beholding a bookstore stuffed to the ceiling with books.

And still they insist on writing them, the man marvels.

"Paul!" a voice bellows from across the street.

I turn around; it's Booth, walking out of Oscar's Bistro with a clutch of his employees.

"Go on ahead!" he yells back at them, crossing the street. "I'll see you all at the store."

"Paul!" He pauses to shakily relight his cigarillo. "Have you given any further thought to the store? The American section."

I shift back and forth on my feet. "Actually, I think – "

"*A new image for America,*" he interrupts. "That's what we need."

He is standing directly before me now, his voice loud and palsied, his sweater a little torn, his cigarillo dying out again. I can't quite look at him through his smudged glasses. I glance over into the emptied Butter Market, over at the entrance to Mark Westwood Books, back at Pemberton's bookshop, and then down at my shoes.

"So what are your plans?" he blurts.

"Actually, we're . . . we're moving."

"You found a house?"

"No, no, we didn't. I mean we're moving . . . back. To the U.S."

"Oh."

"I'm just not ready for Hay yet, I suppose."

"Oh."

And then I fix my gaze on one of the old stone columns of the Butter Market. It is all faintly embarrassing. I find myself thinking about Kate Sanborn, the writer of that unsalable remainder *Hunting Indians in a Taxicab.* While sorting my section at Booth's store, I'd come upon another book by Sanborn, about her move from the big city out to the New England coutryside. It was titled *Adopting an Abandoned Farm.* Later, I came across her next book, published just a few years later: *Abandoning an Adopted Farm.*

"Anyway . . ."

"I'm going to the shop," he says. "You must stay with me next time you are in Hay. We have rooms in the castle, you know. A few that aren't burnt out."

"I'd like that."

"Well, good-bye, then."

I try to smile and I wave wordlessly to him as he shuffles away. And then, I turn on my heel and walk quickly, in no particular direction. Walking down Lion Street brings me to the Bull Ring, and then to Martin Like's office. I don't see anyone in the office, to my relief; and so I lean against the glass and stare mutely at property listings.

Georgian Terraced Town House with stone elevations
under a pitched slate roof
Farm building converted about 9 years ago to character cottage
Victorian Brick and Slate Mid-Terraced Cottage
Attractive Character Town House, Grade II Listed

They are perfectly good houses; Hay is a perfectly good place. And it is Richard Booth's place. Here is a man who, for better or worse, has given his life to a town; who is willing to acquire that most infamous sort of a money pit – a castle – and to live in it and restore it for decades after it burned down. I can hardly even face simple structural work on a cockeyed old pub.

And I guess Booth thinks I'm one of them. But he is British; I am only British in name. They can settle down – and simply *settle,* be content with one's lot in life. But my parents emigrated into a restless society, with few families retaining their members in one town for more than a few decades before dispersing outward. There are no generations of Davies, Beales, Pughs, and Jones where I come from. Not in the Pennsylvania town I grew up in. And not in the next dozen towns I lived in, either.

I open the front door to Pemberton's with trepidation. Diana is in the back, giving a man change for a Hugh Laurie novel.

"Paul! I'm glad to catch you before you go (five pence change, thank you) – did Hazel go over the arrangements with you for the keys and so forth?"

"Yeah. I think that's all squared away."

"Good, good."

I notice a catalog on her desk. "Oh!" I thumb through it. "I guess my book won't be listed in it just yet."

I lay it back down and Diana regards it thoughtfully for a moment.

"I didn't always work in bookstores, you know."

"What?"

"Bookstores. I didn't always work in bookstores. I worked in fashion."

"Really?"

"A long time ago. But, yes – and I didn't live here. I was an assistant to a designer, to – oh, you wouldn't know, you're a man. But he had his studio in Greece at the time." She belatedly marks down the Laurie sale. "I used to travel with him as well, all over the place. It was quite head turning for a young girl. I remember that when we got to New York, there were all these people from *Women's Wear Daily* waiting, and we were whisked off to the Plaza, I think. When I got to my room there, I got undressed, just my nightshirt – long trip and all, I was tired – and made myself a cocktail. Only, I didn't know where to put the glass when I was finished. I hadn't been in these kind of places! I didn't know. I thought it must go on its tray out in the hallway. And so I slipped out the door to leave the tray outside and – click – it locks behind me."

"No."

"Mmm hmm. And I was barely dressed, absolutely *mortified*. I couldn't go down to the lobby and ask for help like that. So I asked people stepping off the elevator, knocked on doors, and people would shut them in my face. I think they thought I was *pros-ti-tute*."

She shakes her head at the memory.

"Well, in any case. So you are leaving. I'm afraid I might not be able to see you off. Did Jennifer tell you?"

"Yes, I think so."

"I'm off to Cardiff. Damned inconvenient."

"I really hope it goes well."

"Yes. I hope so too."

I make my polite farewell and leave with her story still stuck in my head. It is an odd little anecdote, from a past life far from here. But I can't help thinking that she is saying – here, keep this story for me. In case I do not come back.

I have moved thirty-two times and have gone through forty-three roommates, not including a few long-term sofa-crashers. For much of my twenties I went through about four addresses a year, just because I could not decide what I wanted to do with myself – except write, I always knew that – and I didn't know where I wanted to be doing this as yet unknown thing.

I know the *echo,* the sound an apartment makes after you remove your furniture, your frameless futon and blankets, your dirty rug and your shelfloads of books; there is nothing to dampen the sharp click and clomp of heels on the wooden floors, the thud of emptiness on emptiness. You are a tenant in any home, you cannot own it, though you may have a deed that says so. Someone else will live in it after you, as someone did before you, and your last moments here are spent sweeping up trash, patching holes with hasty Spackle, and looking one last time at the hallways and rooms that have been vacated of meaning to you, as empty now as glasses turned upside down to dry.

But – strange – The Apartment at 4 High Town does not echo. It groans with each step, and creaks, but it is that oddest of creatures, a furnished apartment. And so when you leave, there is no real parting of ways: when you look upon it from the doorway, it will look back at you expectantly with its comfy chair and circular rug and electric fireplace, waiting for you, as if you are only to be gone a few minutes down the Londis for a frozen curry.

And it is waiting still when the next man lugs his suitcases up the stairs. He is, I find out later, a minister.

My wife breezes past customs in San Francisco and waits for me at the other side; but I, for once in my life, am coming back to America as a foreigner, and I have to wait in the long foreigner line, squashed between a Turk and an Argentine. I nudge my carry-on bag a few inches ahead whenever the line, improbably as it comes to seem, moves. There is nothing in my carry-on but a massively bubble-wrapped old edition of *Curiosities of Literature* that I was afraid to entrust to anyone else, a few Milkybars, and my *Banvard's Folly* manuscript, now marked up with proofreader's symbols in three or four different hands, and which I cannot bear to have out of my grasp. It is bound for the nearest FedEx drop box, to speed on its way to my editor in New York, and from there to a printer.

My first book.

The line inches ahead, and then it is finally my turn. I hand over my black and gold British passport, and everything is going fine because the immigration official doesn't notice that

"You're American."

"Pardon?"

"Your passport." He peers at my picture and then at me. "Says here, *Montgomery, Pennsylvania*. So you're American."

"I'm traveling on a British passport."

He sighs. "Your parents are British?"

"Yes."

"Diplomats?"

"No."

"And you were born in the U.S.?"

"Yes."

"So you're American."

"Well . . . Yes."

"Where's your passport?"

"Uh . . ." Suddenly I feel my windpipe swelling shut. "I don't know. I lost it. I thought it would be okay to travel back on my British passport. I, um, thought."

He regards me for a moment. "Follow me."

"Uh . . ."

"This way."

I follow, looking around furtively for my wife as she waits on the other side; she has been distracted, though, and she does not see me being led away. My guts begin to slide around inside me, forming into a perfect Windsor knot. I am led to a room built of partition walls; inside are two men and one woman. They are all bigger than me and each has a holstered gun and a clipboard. This does not bode well. A great many dark deeds in this world are perpetrated by people equipped with a gun and a clipboard.

"So you're American."

"Yes?"

"But you don't have a passport."

"No?"

I am shrinking with each syllable, but there is no rabbit hole to slip down, just four partition walls and a table lit by angry fluorescent lighting, and people with guns.

"Hmm."

"I . . . I thought it was okay to travel on my British passport."

"What were you going to do when you got in?"

"Get my passport reissued . . . I guess."

"Yeah," the woman says. "There's the problem. See, we'd have to let you in as a British citizen, but your passport indicates that you're actually American."

"I thought I was both?"

"Not officially. We don't recognize dual citizenship in this country. And if we let you in as British, when we know you're really American" – she raps her clipboard with her knuckles – "we would be, oh, *tacitly* acknowledging your dual citizenship. Which we can't do."

I can feel sweat trickling out of my armpits and down my sides, beneath my shirt. "Oh."

"So you see our dilemma."

"Yes."

She sighs and looks over my passport again, rapping the board a couple more times, as if awaiting a signal in return from the spirit world. I think of my wife and child on the other side, just feet away, waiting for me – Christ! What have I done? They're going to send me back! I have no plan B, nobody and nowhere to go back to . . . what the hell have I done? Jennifer's going to be waiting and waiting for me, not knowing what happened, while some pissed-off British embassy official jams my ass onto a flight back to London, with nothing in my bag but a manuscript and candy bars. How could I have trifled with my own citizenship like this?

"Um," I start, and choke.

She waves her hand and cuts me off. "Listen." She reaches for a rubber stamp. "Look at me."

I look up, fearful. "Yes?"

"I'm going to let you in."

Oh my god.

"I'm going to stamp you as an American in your British passport," she continues. "You are not traveling as a citizen of Britain, as far as I'm concerned. This is an American passport today."

"Okay," I squeak.

"Get your new passport immediately."

"Okay, yes, okay. Okay."

She stamps the passport – hard.

"In the future, I want you to remember that you're not British. You're American."

"Yes." I nod. "I am an American."

She hands my passport back to me.

"Don't ever try to be British again."

I stuff the incriminating document into my pocket.

"Don't worry," I promise. "I won't."

THE END

P.S. Diana is doing fine now.

Acknowledgments

This book is about my life, but my life is about my family. Were it not for Jennifer's love and guidance, this book simply could not have come together at all.

I'd also like to particularly express my gratitude to Marc Thomas, the unheralded fifth Beatle of this story. He's not in it, but he was there and knows it better than anyone else.

As always, I owe much to Dave Eggers. In the fuss over his own writing, he has never really gotten his due as a mentor and publisher to a new generation of writers.

My thanks go out to the many people who unwittingly stumbled into the pages of this book, especially the good citizens of the Kingdom of Hay, starting with the King of Hay himself, Richard Booth. There are too many others to list here, but the least I can do is thank Tim Bent, Mark Thomas of Cable & Wireless, Diana and Julian Blunt, the Ratcliffe family, Martin Like, Mick Brennan, Martin Beales, Christine Cleaton, Derek Addyman, Brian Wiggington, Liz Meres, Sid Wilding, and all the other employees of Booth's . . . book-towners who are now in a book themselves.

I should note here that, unlikely as it sometimes seems to me, the town of Hay-on-Wye is a real place, as are its people and the events of this book. Aliases have been given, though, to several locations and people in the town of Hay.

A big thank-you goes to both my agent, Michelle Tessler, and my editor, Colin Dickerman, who helped make sure that this book saw the light of day.

I owe an artistic debt to the writers whose work inspired and shaped this book: Isaac D'Israeli's *Curiosities of Literature,* James Bailey's *England From a Back-Window,* Andrew Boyd's *Recreations of a Country Parson,* Nicholson Baker's *The Size of Thoughts,* and Edmund Pearson's *Books in Black or Red.* They're mostly out of print now, but I bet you can find them all in Hay. Also, a tip of the hat to the multitude of authors whose works I've quoted and otherwise exhumed in these pages. Someday this book will join you on those dusty shelves, its binding shaken and a little soiled like yours, and we'll all gaze out upon the passing years.

Finally, my sincere thanks to the U.S. government for not deporting me.

Paul Collins is the author of *Banvard's Folly*, and edits the Collins Library imprint of McSweeney's Books. His writing has appeared in *New Scientist, Business 2.0*, and *Cabinet*.

A NOTE ON THE TYPE

This old-style face is named after the Frenchman Robert Granjon, a sixteenth-century letter cutter whose italic types have often been used with the romans of Claude Garamond. The origins of this face, like those of Garamond, lie in the late-fifteenth-century types used by Aldus Manutius in Italy. A good face for setting text in books, magazines, and periodicals.

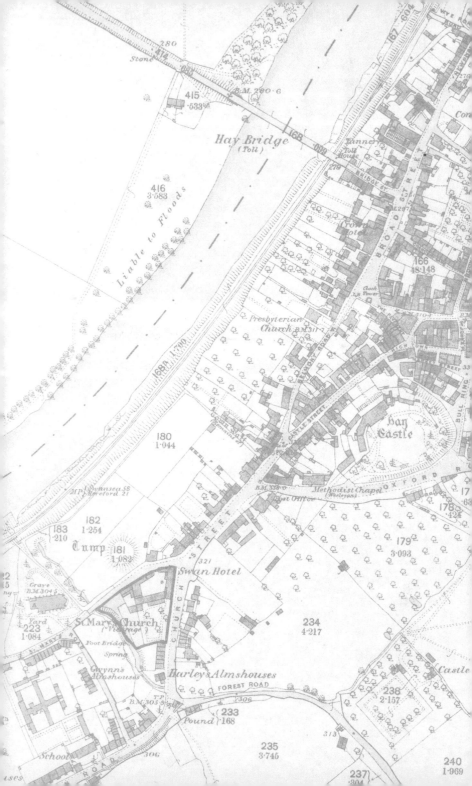